EAT
BRA

JOHN BOSCH
JULIETTE VAN DER MEIJDEN
MAURICE NIO
WIM NIJENHUIS
NATHALIE DE VRIES

ING

ZIL

010 PUBLISHERS
ROTTERDAM

TEXT
WIM NIJENHUIS
DESIGN
MAURICE NIO
TRANSLATION>ENGLISH
JOSEPH VINCENT
TRANSLATION<PORTUGUESE
JULIETTE VAN DER MEIJDEN
EDITORIAL ADVICE
MICHAEL SPEAKS

PHOTOGRAPHIC MATERIAL & TEXTS
JOHN BOSCH, EVERT CROLS, JERRY VAN EYCK, MICHAEL VAN GESSEL, PETER HOPMAN, HUUB JUURLINK, BRANIMIR MEDIC, JULIETTE VAN DER MEIJDEN, MAURICE NIO, WIM NIJENHUIS, TON SALMAN, NATHALIE DE VRIES, ENNO ZUIDEMA

FINANCIAL SUPPORT
THE NETHERLANDS FOUNDATION OF FINE ARTS, DESIGN AND ARCHITECTURE, AMSTERDAM, AND THE NETHERLANDS ARCHITECTURE FUND, ROTTERDAM

ISBN 90 6450 364 8

CONTENTS

popu
5.68

1. Vehement Brazil. Coruscating on the coast beneath a resplendent blue sky lies Clube Costa Brava, surrounded by lush and saturated green. The soil is red and dense, the sea blue. The sun shines ardently on the beach; the heat of the climate is fierce. With crackling forks of lightning, thunderstorms rend the sky open and the rain gushes down like a waterfall. Vivid are the colours of the people, and even more vivid are those of the fauna (parrots and birds of paradise).

2. My initial fear of being mugged in the street pales into insignificance against my surreptitious expectation receiving a gift. This is a generous country, not only in its agriculture (coffee, sugar cane), its mineral wealth (gold, emeralds), its tropical fruit and of course the lusciousness of its vegetation and its women, but in time. If there is anything which Brazil has in surplus, which it squanders recklessly, then it is that worthless commodity, time.

3. Time is filled up with waiting, and waiting is filled up with activities that go along with waiting.

4. Everywhere there are soulkissing couples, immersed in love at warp minus 6. Everywhere there are questions that must wait fifteen minutes for an answer; early mor-

ning shreds of mist that lick warily at the city; sugary cocktails you can only drink very slowly, in tiny sips; brown beans that simmer on a burner the whole day long.

5. In the evening, a pigeon with its neck twisted to one side hobbles along the sand of Copacabana beach. Probably hit by a car. As the bird slowly expires against the brilliant white backdrop of surf bathed in hundreds of spotlights, I get the feeling that the tableau has been contrived especially for my benefit some voodoo ritual to warn me that I am not welcome in this paradise.

6. Rio de Janeiro means 'River of January'. The Portuguese thought the bay of Guanabara was a river.

7. The 'Independent Republic of Roçinha' houses 300,000 inhabitants. It is not on the map. Roçinha runs wild over the hills around Barra da Tijuca like some post-apocalyptic mutation of the rain forest. Like the rain forest, it is virtually inaccessible to the police and the fire service. But not to the satellite: aerial dishes flaunt shamelessly on the roofs of the unbroken masses of building.

8. Along the Atlantic coast in the direction of São Conrado, the city grows as a plaited skein of rich and

poor. Condomínios, walled neighbourhoods, are built amid almost pristine greenery; they are walled because that is how they do things in the USA. The poor soon follow, for arrival of the condomínio means jobs. In some instances the poor lived there first. At places along the loveliest parts of the coastal strip, their settlements were cleared to make room for walled and mostly high-rise suburbs. The purchase price of a dwelling in a condomínio may reach as much as 1.5 million US dollars.

9. On a balcony looking out over Copacabana, Niemeyer stands, corpulent and self-satisfied, dreaming of immortality.

10. The image of Rio de Janeiro is dominated by its landscape. The drama of the peaks and rocky outcrops is breathtaking as they fuse with the coast, or march solemnly out into the sea. Hills and outcrops remain unbuilt above the 100 metres level because of the expected difficulty of supplying piped drinking water. It is this that gave rise to the 3300-hectare Floresta da Tijuca, the forest that stretches out under the eternal gaze of the world-renowned figure of Christ. It was also a constraint that forced the city to grow exclusively along the narrow, level coastal strips. There

you can see many blocks of flats with bases like mangrove roots; and there too you experience the paradoxical diminutiveness of the architecture that is so typical of Rio de Janeiro. Mercilessly, the flats and office blocks are subordinated to the geological formations of mountains and rocks, to the undulating immensity of the ocean and to the blue dome of the sky – in short, to matters that are dedicated to infinite slowness.

11. When the poor occupy a patch of ground that is still unbuilt, or, more importantly, where building is forbidden, it generally means the start of a favela, an illicit district. I was given to understand that Rio has over 150 favelas with a total population of one million. Brazilian law states that you are not obliged to pay rent or tax if your home is not finished. The favela house – or, rather, hovel – is hence never finished! There is no end to its building. On closer acquaintance the favela proves to be an autonomous community capable of satisfying all its own needs. It has its own regulations and laws, as well as its own mayor. There are also unwritten rules of conduct that everyone obeys: for example, never get in the way of the traficantes, the drugs barons. But above all the favela is a condition of anarchy. Bundles of

power cables, telephone lines and water pipes, held together with tie-wraps and tape, snake through the settlement. There are neither sewers nor garbage collection services.

12. Rio contains the world's biggest football stadium, the Maracanã. It has a capacity of 200,000 people. So it could contain the entire population of a city like Eindhoven. It is by far the most important building in the city.

13. Viewed from the Sugar Loaf the clandestine neighbourhoods of the poor, known here as favelas, nestle in the mountains like glaciers. It is as though they could come tumbling down at any moment. Nobody would build in such places in the mountains of Europe, for it is in these dips that avalanches and mudslides seek their course. And the ground beneath the favela is itself unstable. That is why the legal building developers have taken no interest in these sites. Aside from the dubious legal status of the favela, it is founded literally on precarious ground. And once the latter is loosened by heavy rainfall and starts slipping down the mountain, the poor are likely to be swept down the slope with all their goods and chattels onto the wealthy districts lying directly beneath them. Al-

REAL

though this geophysical tension is a genuine expression of the principle of seduction that we find throughout Brazilian culture, the danger gave the authorities a pretext to clear the favelas. They continued doing so into the sixties, but in the nineties such policies are no longer feasible. The clandestine neighbourhood is instead given legal recognition and eventually the soil on which it rests is stabilized. So, at last, the poor have gained some kind of reliable foothold.

14. As irony would have it, the favelas often cluster on the city's most attractive locations. Where the apartments and villas of the better-off are generally sited on the flank of a hill with a prospect of the ocean, you will generally find a favela above it occupying an even lovelier location and with an even more panoramic view. The favelas are not concentrated in a single area. On the contrary, they have metastasized throughout the body of the city. Sometimes the boundary between a wealthy neighbourhood and an adjoining favela is contrastive in the extreme. Indeed, you come across situations where the view from the windows of a luxury home is completely filled by an enormous favela.

Curiously, the favelas are such an accepted presence nowadays that

they may be considered part of the urban culture. They look awfully untidy, of course, but hey, this is Brazil. The favela has become so familiar that the Brazilians cannot bear to part with them. The city authorities are busy finding ways to uphold their chaotic pattern of building. The neighbourhoods are provided with sewers, and attempts are made to collect garbage and to lay on legitimate mains electricity and water. Even municipal buses rumble through them. Occasionally people try to improve the living circumstances in the favelas by renovation. And sometimes they even liven a new housing development by designing it to resemble a favela.

15. The district of Copacabana is built on sand. Construction began in 1903 on the basis of an urban plan of French origin. The district consists of a grid extending over the narrow strip of land between the mountains and the beach. The dimensions of the streets bear no resemblance to those of 19th century French colonial urban designs in Africa and Asia. The relatively small scale is more reminiscent of British town planning or of the streets of Manhattan.

The original building style of Copacabana is Art Nouveau. That is hardly surprising considering the

period in which it was established. The choice of Art Nouveau rather than neo-classicism is connected with the original function and placing of the district. Copacabana was originally built as a suburb in rural seaside surroundings, about 8 kilometres from the centre of the city on which it depended. Its position was thus rather like – to take a Dutch example – that of Zandvoort in relation to Amsterdam.

The Art Nouveau low-rise buildings began disappearing rapidly in the forties, when Copacabana acquired an international reputation as a seaside and gambling resort. It was replaced by medium-rise in Art Deco. In the sixties, the district started going into a cultural decline. Copacabana lost its premier status to the adjacent seaside district of Ipanema. This suburb, too, had been built up around a traditional French-style grid of streets of relatively small dimensions, and like Copacabana it is built on the sands of the beach. Meanwhile, the face of Copacabana has undergone a further transformation. The Art Deco has given way to a kind of neutral, profit-driven high-rise, which expresses above all the high land prices of the area. Only the Copacabana Palace Hotel still recalls the district's former glory. The rectangular plots marked off by the grid are generally fringed by this neutral,

quasi-modernist high-rise. Behind it, some remnants of the low-rise and medium-rise of the earlier periods are still to be found.

The metamorphoses of Copacabana are typical of the areas of Rio de Janeiro that were laid out according to the rules of European town planning. The centre of Rio has undergone three major changes of face in the last hundred years, transforming it from nineteenth century Eclecticism to Art Deco, and from Art Deco to the neutral modernism of the sixties. Nowadays postmodernism is on the ascendant, but it is flanked by attempts to repair the existing urban fabric. What is striking here is the contrast – a whole 'restored' late nineteenth century street cowers in the shadow of a post-modern giant.

The value and the significance of Copacabana are determined by the wish to dwell in the countryside close to a city, which underlies suburbanization all over the world. As the suburb becomes increasingly integrated with its mother city over time, the value of the location is increasingly determined by the quality of the available public amenities. When the cult status of Copacabana declined during the sixties, the local authorities tried to stem the process by widening the esplanade, a scheme that also aimed to make the adjacent properties less

vulnerable to damage by storms and high tides. The project was designed by the famous Brazilian landscape architect Roberto Burle Marx.

The unusually wide esplanade is divided into a number of parallel strips. Starting from the ocean, we first cross the beach to a pedestrian path paved in a waving pattern of tiles. The pattern is said to originate from a Portuguese motif. Next to the walking path, there is a track for cyclists, skaters, speed-walkers and joggers. This is followed by a roadway for motor vehicles of approximately four lanes wide, then a central reservation, and then another four-lane vehicle road. The central reservation contains greenery and fuel stations. Between the latter carriageway and the facades of the adjacent properties, there is a generous footpath elaborately paved in mosaic patterns and adorned with pieces of greenery of varying placing and design. Unlike the walking path adjacent to the beach, the central reservation and the pavement offer a certain amount of shade.

The motifs in the mosaic paving, which can alas only be seen from a height, are taken from native and ethnic art. Burle Marx carried out extensive research into forms and meanings that could provide a solid anchorage for the Modern Style – an anchorage, indeed, for like Frank Lloyd Wright, the Brazilian Mo-

derns wished to regionalize the Modern Style and appropriate it to their national tradition. A necessary precondition for this was to achieve an integration with historic local forms. In Brazil, these local forms were threefold: native Indian art, Negro art and the historic art of European immigrants. The Brazilian Modern Movement favoured using the expressionist idiom to unite the Brazilian Baroque with the two ethnic art forms, and to provide them with a vital, energetic principle: the Brazilian Soul.

For Burle Marx and his fellow spirits, the Brazilian Soul had a symbolic implication in the most literal sense. Energy could be gathered from the death of the past to fuel a new start. The Brazilian culture of the fifties and sixties was thus a thoroughly optimistic one. It was a culture that survived on hope, and it took upon itself the duty of fostering hope by means of its works of art. In terms of a strategy of hope, the Esplanade of Copacabana is a highly successful design. You experience an 'awakening to the future' such as you might experience when listening to good music, and in this awakening you also sense a resonance of the forms of the past – of African slaves, of the Brazilian Indians and of the Brazilian Baroque. But now the whole thing gives a rather dated and im-

poverished impression, because its symbolic meaning has more to do with poetry than with status.

16. I am determined to spend my last day in Brazil on the beach. I have decided to keep things simple and restrict my choices. Rio has such an enormous selection of beaches that I sometimes experience the city as one big beach, interrupted only occasionally by some or other favela. But there are two beaches right in the vicinity, Copacabana and Ipanema, both of which I have studied closely and have lodged deeply in my imagination. Let me put it this way. Food and drink? Both beaches have coconut milk and vendors who come along with canned drinks. McDonalds on Ipanema and Bob's on Copacabana. Sunshine? Yes, loads. Surf? Copacabana: yeah, maybe... Ipanema: yes. Views? From Ipanema, a favela; from Copacabana, the Sugar Loaf. Sports? Surfing on Ipanema beach, on Copacabana plenty of aerobics, beach-footvolleyball and jogging oldies. I saw a roller-skater on the cycle path at both resorts. Fresh air? Copacabana is grey with smog, but Ipanema is miles better. Night life? Nothing going at Ipanema, except perhaps as a place for gays to meet up. At Copacabana, there's the 'Hello' disco, where you have to

1,50

watch out because they are reputed to spike the drinks there. The beach is not the place for evening entertainment; there are better venues for that. Copacabana has mostly streetwalkers at night. Tourists? Only Copacabana has them. Ipanema is the place to be when you're single in Rio. Malicious delight? In Ipanema, being cool's the thing. In Copacabana, you can laugh your head off. So I think Copacabana has the edge. Ambiance? I'm not sure, but I prefer Copacabana. Babewatch? In Copacabana, rien de tout (in my age group, at least). In Ipanema – YOU BET!

17. Very impressive. That's the least I could say about Edifício Sede-Petrobrás in the centre of Rio. A lucky shot. A bit bulky, but touché, this 1968 design by the architects Roberto Luiz Gandolfi, José H. Sanchotene, Abraão Assad en Luiz Fortes Netto. The colossal structure can be seen from miles away, but at close quarters its enormousness is striking. It's only when you stand right underneath it that it's clear just how absurdly huge those notches are. Then you also understand that they have to be there to allow daylight and fresh air into the offices. Each recess proves on closer inspection to contain a garden; and these were designed by no-one less than the Brazilian master,

Roberto Burle Marx. What a pity nobody uses them. All praise for the experiment. Besides the facade cladding, two thirds of which consists of the external aluminium slats you see everywhere in Brazil, there are narrow-slatted metal Venetian sunblinds between the double glazing of the windows.

18. I have plundered the mini-bars in the hotel rooms and I have broken into the swimming pool area on the hotel roof.

19. Modernism in all its facets has made its mark on Rio de Janeiro. But there is a clear difference between the successive generations of modernism. As one strip of beach and shore after another was brought into development from the late 19th century onwards – Copacabana, Ipanema, Leblon, São Conrado and Barra de Tijuca – an anonymous variant of modernism eventually gained the upper hand here too. The high density of development has left little room for large, detached buildings. On the other side of the city, where it borders on the bay, there is a vast area of suburban development and fused villages, in which a building style pitched at the middle classes is better represented.

20. Rio de Janeiro has recently experienced a revival in urban plan-

ning. Inspired by European examples, the city authorities decided to take an intensive, firm-handed approach to public space in various districts of the city. The Rio Cidade (Rio City) program not only aims to refurbish the streets, squares and parks, but also aims to raise the standard of maintenance and management, and where necessary to institute total renovation or new construction of underground infrastructure such as sewers, water mains and electricity cables. Many public investments in Rio have been directed at maintaining and improving the existing city fabric.

21. Brazil does not have an alcoholic beverage with an alcohol percentage between 5 (beer/choppe) and 50 (cachaça).

22. Praça Tiradentes. Braking sharply, my hostess brought her limousine to a halt with the bumper in a heap of rubbish. Money disappeared into the coarseskinned fist of a random pauper. We hurried across the dilapidated square and ascended, relieved, the goldilluminated Art Deco steps of the samba dance hall.

23. In the morning at eight I swam in the ocean. Then I went for a walk along the breakers. More people were walking than lying there. That

night I slept alone in a hotel room for the second time in my life.

24. Unemployment and intense sociability. Transparently to the passerby, a mother washes her child.

25. Gelatinous concupiscence. They act and think in the same way as they dance, undulating, languid and slow. Not because everything runs slower here (on the contrary, time seems to pass more quickly) but because time has become a fluid substance that is absorbed by the body.

26. My travelling companions hide their currency and documents under their clothes, in money belts they bought especially for this trip. I think of my clumsy shoulder-bag and feel a little uneasy.

27. Kilo restaurants / Por Kilo.

28. Ipanema. The women were looking so intently at my crotch that I bought a roll of peppermints and slid them into the trouser pocket of my lightweight suit.

29. The curve of the girl's bust was isomorphous with the flanks of the Sugar Loaf and her lips captured the horizon of the Atlantic Ocean in their parting. In the distance: the brandnew museum in Niterói by Oscar Niemeyer.

popu
2.06

1. Belo Horizonte was founded in 1894. It was meant to be the capital city of the wealthy province of Minas Gerais. Its plan takes the form of a rectangular grid of streets with a diagonal grid of avenues cutting across it at 45°. This scheme was derived without further ado from P. Ch. L'Enfant's 1791 plan for Washington D.C. That was the first design that gave expression to bourgeois-agricultural values with which people here in Belo feel an affinity. In the surrounding region, people mine iron, gold, diamonds, manganese, bauxite and rock crystal, cultivate coffee and raise cattle.

2. The traditional local dish is tutu à mineira. The recipe consists chiefly of pork and couve, a green vegetable bearing some resemblance to spinach, with an addition of the famous tutu, a thick bean sauce made by boiling a mixture of black beans and manioc meal. Many of the local dishes of Belo Horizonte originate from the mule trains and expeditions of the Bandeirantes in the eighteenth century. They relied on food which could be preserved for lengthy periods, which was uncomplicated to prepare and did not require any

fancy ingredients.

3. Belo Horizonte must be approached from the south. As you approach by car over the lovely hills of the Serra do Espinhaço, you suddenly cross a ridge and the whole city stretches out before you. It is a spectacular sight. A sea of skyscrapers, favelas and industrial zones fills an enormous bowl formed by the surrounding hills. Conversely, the spiky, rust-coloured skyline of the Serra do Espinhaço can be seen from any point in the centre of the city. Hence the city's name – beautiful horizon. The shape of the skyline is gradually changing, however, because the open-cast mining operations continually gnaw away at the 'iron breast' of the mountains.

4. Anthropophagy, abaporu, cannibalism. You don't go to bed with someone, you 'give'(dar) or you 'eat'(comer) someone. A woman can never 'eat' a man. Her gift is to give. Only 'piranhas' eat men. A piranha is a carnivorous fish, and it is also a woman who treats men as paying customers. The Portuguese once sent a bishop to Brazil. The Indians made a tasty meal of him. In Manifesto Ant-

MEDICO
224·4407
kit

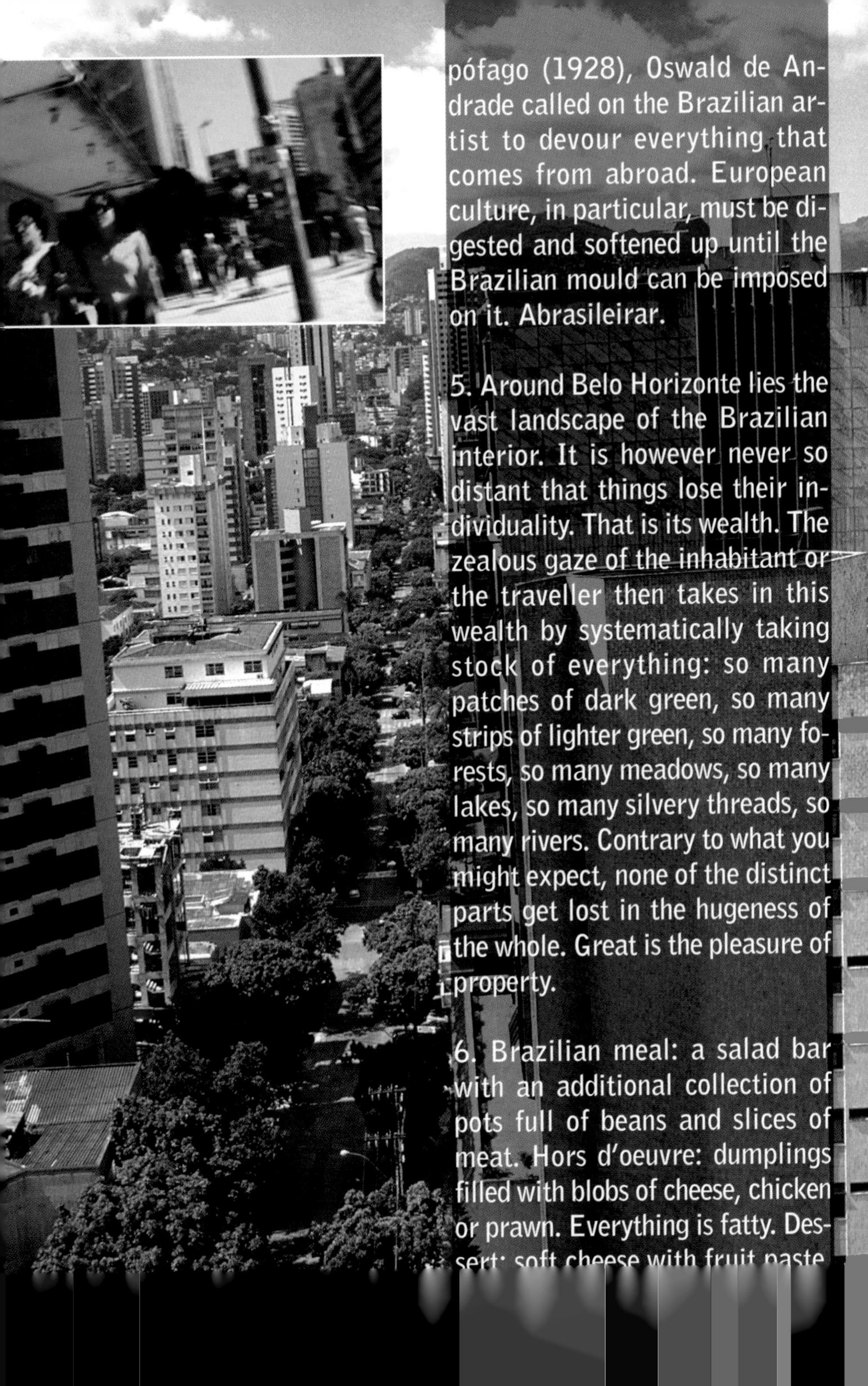

pófago (1928), Oswald de Andrade called on the Brazilian artist to devour everything that comes from abroad. European culture, in particular, must be digested and softened up until the Brazilian mould can be imposed on it. Abrasileirar.

5. Around Belo Horizonte lies the vast landscape of the Brazilian interior. It is however never so distant that things lose their individuality. That is its wealth. The zealous gaze of the inhabitant or the traveller then takes in this wealth by systematically taking stock of everything: so many patches of dark green, so many strips of lighter green, so many forests, so many meadows, so many lakes, so many silvery threads, so many rivers. Contrary to what you might expect, none of the distinct parts get lost in the hugeness of the whole. Great is the pleasure of property.

6. Brazilian meal: a salad bar with an additional collection of pots full of beans and slices of meat. Hors d'oeuvre: dumplings filled with blobs of cheese, chicken or prawn. Everything is fatty. Dessert: soft cheese with fruit paste

In the morning breakfast has the same composition, but is supplemented with slices of melon and pineapple and sweet rolls.

Never overload your plate! Never eat it all up clean! Prolong the act of eating as long as possible, that is the art. A large plate heaped with a single meal is called a 'prepared plate'. You can only get it in the cheapest of restaurants.

7. In Belo Horizonte, you are in a real city. It can rain like home, you can be stuck in the traffic for hours (just road works), it has just one city centre. But it has magnificent road intersections where the diagonal avenues meet the orthogonal streets. These corners are marked by special buildings with distinctive architectural designs. The scale of Belo Horizonte's centre feels immediately familiar, almost like home. There are none of those awful shopping malls but real shopping streets. It has tree-lined streets and streets with pavements, and streets that sometimes run to a dead end.

8. Brazil eats. Eats itself. Eats up its inhabitants. In twenty-five

Toma
Cynar
que dá.
CYNAR
LONG NECK
BRAHMA
$ 0,90
Coca-Cola

years, they will eat us up. Eat my brains, now. To match this, with anything convincing at least, you have to come up with a cannibalistic theory – a theory that eats a way for itself, mentally and physically, through the immense country.

You get the impression here that the cities are not there for the people, but the people are there for the cities. They are fodder for the Brazilian metropolis. What is a city-dweller here? Yes, someone who gets eaten. And, on the horizon, there is always fresh fodder on its way in the form of the favelas.

9. The people have subtly armed themselves against the cannibalism of their cities. They devour time, they devour the sun and they devour their own consciousness in response to the hectic gluttony of the space around them. Never have I seen so many unconscious acts, so many people whose thoughts drift off, who live and speak on automatic pilot, who live in a slower time zone. What was it the Brazilian town planner said? Oh yes, there is either action without planning, or planning wit-

without action. Here, thinking and doing are worlds apart.

10. Belo Horizonte consists of buildings that have either 2 or 20 stories. There is nothing in between. This balance is being disturbed by increasing high-rise building. Developers are trying to reverse this process by building sub-centres with shopping malls outside the city. The establishment of condominiums is forbidden. Nonetheless some private groups have somehow succeeded in closing off streets that were already cul-de-sacs. (In the superquadras of Brasília, there is no need to seal the entrances. There the city spends heavily on maintaining the public domain, as it is obliged to do by the national government.) Despite the barricaded cul-de-sacs, Belo Horizonte is still the best city in which to ramble around at leisure.

11. Pure and aesthetic – that is the Brazilian as long as he is alone. As soon as two of them are together, they make a mess of it. On a first acquaintance people kiss, on the second they embrace. Nonetheless, the Brazilians are more reserved and courteous than

many a North European.

A pity that Brazilian men look so inconspicuous.

The strength of the Brazilian does not reside solely in the hips.

In the Brazilian home, the kitchen is the most important space. It has to be large and central.

12. Oscar Niemeyer's Banco do Estado de Minas Gerais is exceptionally beautiful. The buildings stands on one of those sites with a corner of 45°. Brises-soleils on one side of the acute angle and an open glass structure on the other side – very well done. The arbitrary way the air-conditioning units are stuck onto the building gives an extra dimension to its texture.

Edifício Niemeyer on Praça de Liberdade (Liberation Square) has an organic ground plan. The free use of brise-soleils makes the building's facade as sculptural as a rustling evening dress.

13. Europe as against Brazil. Haute cuisine as against cannibalism. The luxury of choice and reflection as against the primary

need to control and absorb. The refinement of the well-considered concept as against the crudity of immediate consumption.

In one respect Brazil always hits the mark: the serving of food. Waiters serve us with one kind of meat after another, at insane speed. It is though they plan to fatten us up and then... devour us.

Brazilians love sweet things.

14. Following one of the roads that lead from the centre of Belo Horizonte to the surrounding countryside, we came across a landscape project of considerable size. It centres around the artificial Lake Pampulha. The man responsible for this prestige project in the forties is Juscelino Kubitchek, then mayor of Belo Horizonte – yes, the very one who was later to build Brasília! This aficionado of modern architecture put his friend Niemeyer to work around the lake to design a number of buildings for recreational purposes, including a yacht club, a tennis club, a restaurant, a dance hall, a church and a casino. It was for the benefit of the

bourgeoisie of Belo Horizonte.

15. Figura serpentinata. The women move gracefully, for they believe in the sacrality of gesture. The head stays vertical, moving serenely back and forth along an imaginary horizontal line. The hips and lower back form a supple link with the moving feet. The result is a sinuous pulsation combined with a free movement of the extremities in loose and endless variations. The same principle is followed by the Edifício Niemeyer flats in Belo Horizonte, where the rooftop penthouse is held between two curves, one a wide, capricious circumscription of the other.

16. In 1923, the poet Mario de Andrade challenged the painter Tarsila do Amaral with the cry, 'Abandon Paris! Tarsila! Tarsila! Tarsila! Tarsila! Come to the virgin forest.' In his 1928 Manifesto Antropófago, Oswald de Andrade wrote, 'Before the Portuguese discovered Brazil, Brazil discovered happiness.' In Giovanni Boccaccio's Decamerone, 1353, the preacher Cipolla astonished his congregation by producing a feather from the wing of the Arch-

angel Gabriel. Actually, it came from a parrot. In 1894, the original inhabitants of the impoverished village Curral d'El Rey were moved out to make room the for building of Belo Horizonte.

17. The Museu de Arte on Avenida Otacílio Negrão de Lima was built in the forties to a design by Oscar Niemeyer. It was originally a casino. Its reflection in the waters of Lake Pampulha symbolizes the monumental value that this building has for the inhabitants of Belo Horizonte. In stylistic respects, it is perhaps a hybrid. The principles of functional architecture predominate on the outside, while the interior, with its large, theatrical spaces, its illusionistic perspectives in the mirrored walls and its sensually curved ramps, recalls the fundamentals of the 'Barocco Mineiro'.

18. Shops and stalls full of esoteric literature abound. Nothing is certain in Brazil. Everything is predestined. You are absolutely certain in the morning about things that you see in a different light that same afternoon. That is why my Dutch directness and decisiveness are inconvenient quali-

Casablanca
POLICIA
MILITAR
ARAGEM PRIVA

ties to have in Brazil. They don't achieve anything.

In the Netherlands, we usually aim to achieve synthesis, integration and compromise. None of these attributes were to be heard in the lectures we attended by Brazilian architects and designers. Direct questions such as 'Where do you go from here?' received puzzled but polite attention. Then the respondent just recited the facts again.

19. I begin to realize that the extremes I was looking forward to before I set out on my journey are simply the consequences of a society in which everything is permitted. Every excrescence, whether positive or negative, has a chance to develop. There is no levelling out here.

Graça Aranha says that, in Brazil, culture and nature are separated according to the following scheme. Portuguese: artificiality and melancholy. African slaves:

intentions, this motion is absorbed in the logic of behaviour and everyday gesture. Every leap forward is thus brought down and every acceleration is braked. Epidemic versus democratic. It is not what suits the people that counts here, but what passes through them.

The indolentia is not melancholic but a little cynical. Malandro, Exu. Not nostalgia but disdain for all values. No history and no historical destination. It wishes for nothing from the past and knows nothing of the future. Personal enterprise is suspect, for the world is a game.

21. Belo Horizonte is a small provincial town by Brazilian standards. It has only 2.5 million inhabitants. Ronaldo was born here. At the airport, a Belgian builder who had been staying in Belo repairing factories damaged by the rain told me, 'Belo is paradise!' Not for work, but for leisure. 'The women here are fantastic!' There are 2,187,500 women and 312,500 men in Belo Horizonte; a ratio of 7 to 1. 'Incredible, seven women to every man.' Belo Horizonte, delicious city, lovely Belo,

Graaaande Kaiser
Kaiser
Kaiser
REAGE BRASIL
REAGE BRASIL

mmmm, so sweet, sweet, soft Belo, ah, grrr, aaah, Belo, Bello Bello, divine, breathtaking, far out. With acknowledgements to the Ciao Ciao Jumping Bar.

22. Going for a stroll, we exit the hotel and cross straight over the Avenida Afonso Pena and turn left in the direction of Praça Sete de Setembro. This Avenida starts in the north-west at Praça Rodaviária, the square with the bus-station which is also the starting point of the road to Pampulha. From there it stretches south-eastwards in a perfectly straight line to a point far in the outskirts. In the middle of the city, the Avenida is flanked on its north-east side by the Parque Municipal, and on the other side by the nearest thing to a central square, Praça Afonso Arinos. Here, Avenida Alvares Cabral, Avenida Augusto de Lima, Avenida João Pinheiro and Rua Goiás all meet.

23. Owing to paranoia and the fact that the Real is worth roughly one US Dollar, everybody in the group is continually short of money. Brazilian cash dispensers eschew European credit cards.

ARA

A little Brazilian girl at an open-air bar offers me a tiny home-made doll stuffed with flour, the kind you can squeeze in you hand. After lengthy bargaining, I end up paying far too much for it. Shortly afterwards, a big Dutch boy squeezes the doll too hard and bursts it. Exactly 350 hours later and 350 kilometres away, I meet an adult Brazilian girl who is the spitting image of that doll. I would like to squeeze her, but I hold back in case she too is stuffed with flour.

24. It is pleasant to be in the shade of the Parque Municipal on the pavement, which must be a good 10 metres wide. The exorbitant dimensions of Avenida Afonso Pena shrink the skyscrapers of the international banks on the other side to the size of cottages. The openness of the space allows a fresh breeze to blow. There are countless carts with soft drinks and ice-cream. We turn left just before Praça Sete de Setembro and enter Rua Dos Tamoios. Tempted by the crafts market (artesanato), we turn into Rua Rio de Janeiro. We pass through flowers, leather goods, polished and rough semi-precious stones, hand-woven

LIMPA

precious stones, hand-woven blankets, jewellery and sentimental paintings and climb to the shopping centre of Rua Dos Tupis.

25. Somnambulism is the ability to avoid hyperwakefulness, a skill which is commanded by the climate.

When you drive through the hinterland of Brazil following the sluggish curves of the immense mountain landscape with your sleepy eyes, it penetrates to you that the cities of this country are absurd, inimitable hyperconcentrations, explosions of people, cars, masonry and asphalt. They resemble the countless termite mounds which dot the hills like little volcanic eruptions. It is as though they came into being during some unguarded moment while the landscape took a little snooze.

26. Walking beneath the foliage of Rua Rio de Janeiro, we cross Avenida Augusto da Lima near the peak of the hill. At the intersection, blocks of flats tower above the generally low-rise building, whose stuccoed, windowless side walls are painted with co-

Brazilian motifs. We continue our walk up to Rua Dos Guajajaras and turn left towards Avenida Alvares Cabral. Here, between the crowns of the trees, we can see the effect of the alternation of high-rise and low-rise buildings and painted side walls at an intersection with diagonal streets. We finally descend through the shade of the palm trees of Praça Afonso Arinos to the hotel on Avenida Afonso Pena.

27. It gives a liberating sensation to realize that the Brazilians have no taste and are uninterested in anything but knick-knacks and kitsch. In European eyes at least. They have mastered the art of mixing everything together. Religion, art, architecture, music and literature – the cocktail is their supreme good.

At the point where Brazil, Paraguay and Argentina meet, the singer moved with the lethargic gesture of the quick, quick, slow. After three steps her tightlyclad body came to rest. She let forth with her voice and brought her feet together, her wide skirt swishing for four bars. The flower in her hair flashed jauntily.

popu
1.67

Empty, remorselessly empty is the Chapadão, the plateau of Brazil's interior. Only the moon is emptier. Godforsaken, devilish ocean. Heaving gently, the hills roll endlessly one after another beneath the fierce blue of a scorching sky. The red soil is covered with tormented, twisted scrubland, pathetically attenuated by the cruel surroundings. Full of flies, mosquitoes, ants and termites, thousands of inaccessible kilometres stretch out under the leering gaze of jealous vultures.

This is the homeland of the caboclo, the new primitive, the 'fallen' European in whose veins there flows the blood of Indians and Negroes. Amid the timelessness of the most recent stone age, 'magical' forces swing him to and fro. Black angels have shackled him to an inhospitable nature. Never has the word of the Redeemer awoken him, or if it has, he has forgotten it. Stupefied by an age-old nostalgia (saudade), he floats like driftwood over the plateau without ever reaching the horizon. Spurred by a natural environment that does not allow him to bond with land or locality, he trudges on barefoot, a stranger to himself and a stranger in an inimical world, in single file. Clad in a cotton shirt he sits on his mule; he can stand on one spot for hours.

Here, the aroma of an unself-

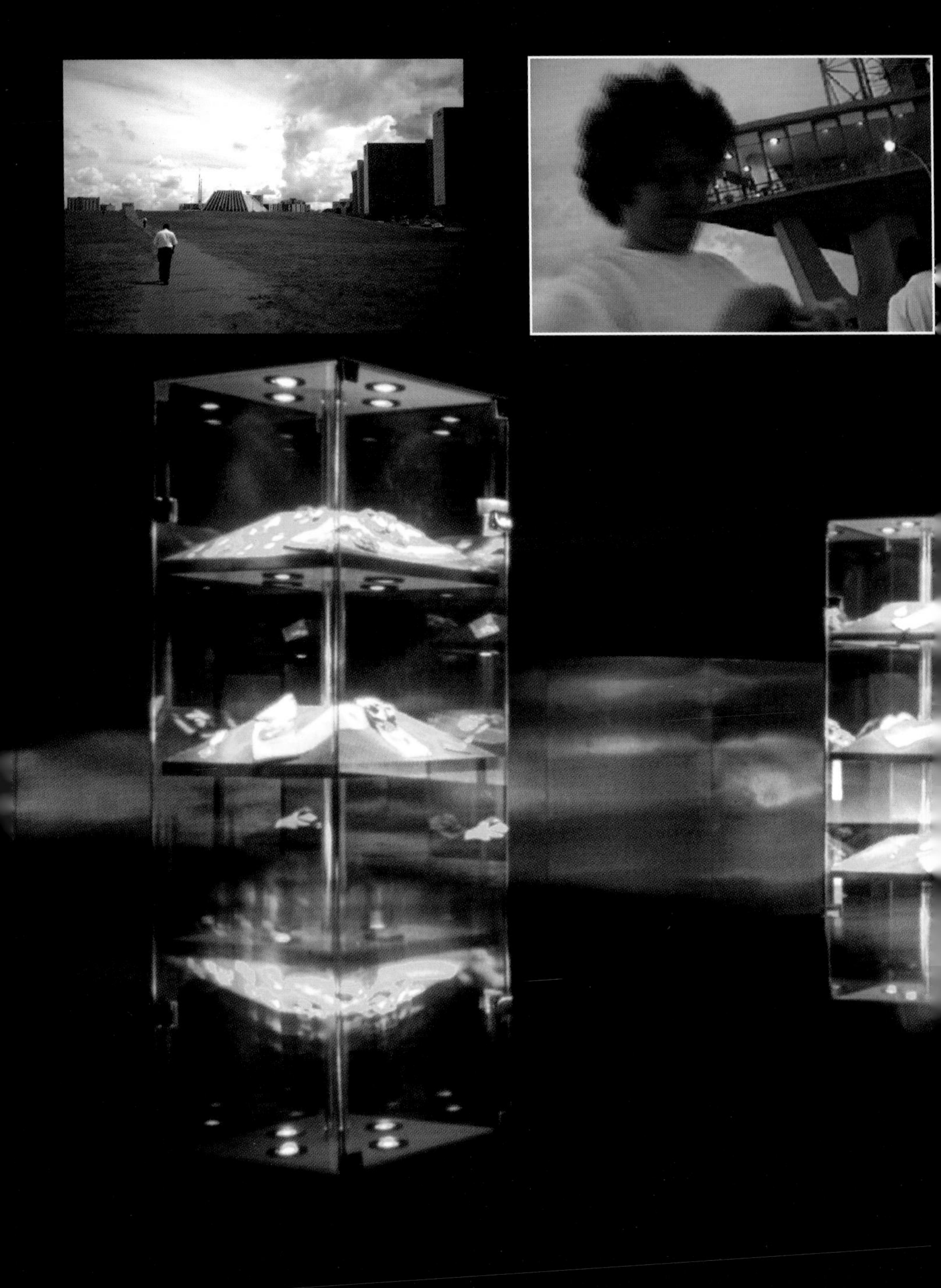

conscious time wafts towards us. Perhaps it is the shadow of paradise, an LSD trip.

In 1954, the Chapadão was charted from the air. Finally, for the first time in 200 years, its inaccessibility was violated. On the 2nd of October 1956, a military plane landed on the provisional airfield. Proudly, a sign with the name Brasília now gleamed in the sun. President Juscelino Kubitchek, engineer Israel Pinheiro, town planner Lúcio Costa and architect Oscar Niemeyer took their first steps on the Chapadão. Soon, the airfield was expanded. Air travel was the only link to the civilized world. The first workmen, the first loads of cement, the first building machinery, the first building materials, food and drink, everything had to be flown in. In the five years Brasília was under construction, President Kubitchek spent most of his time up in the air, his head in a permanent cloud, so transitory as to be unrecognizable without his aviator's helmet, entering or alighting from a helicopter. The presidential palace in Brasília is, too, borne on wings, albeit the wings of angels. The Ministério da Aeronáutica was the first to move from Rio de Janeiro to Brasília. Then the population came pouring in, airlifted from the major cities. In April 1960, six thousand

extra taxi drivers were flown over from Rio. When Brasília was inaugurated on the twenty-first of April, all the appetizers and drinks were flown in directly from Rio together with a 40-man big band.

During the decades before the building of Brasília, the modern life of Brazil had been carried by air. Flying was the favoured of escaping the suffocating provincialism of the late-colonial culture of the main cities. Gifted artists and intellectuals flew to Paris so often that the French capital could, without exaggeration, be called their second home. The height of intercontinental propellor-set snobbery was to have ones laundry done in Paris. It is worth recalling the two large projects realized in the thirties by the group of modern architects around Costa: the seaplane airport in the bay of Rio de Janeiro, and the Santos Dumont airport, named after the Brazilian aviation pioneer. Modern Brazil, that was flying – the upward leap, the flight forward... political kinetics.

If we look at Brasília with the neutral gaze of the designer and lose ourselves in its formal details and all those other matters of morphology, it is all too easy for us to misunderstand the conditions under which urban planning has been perpetrated here. We are unaware then

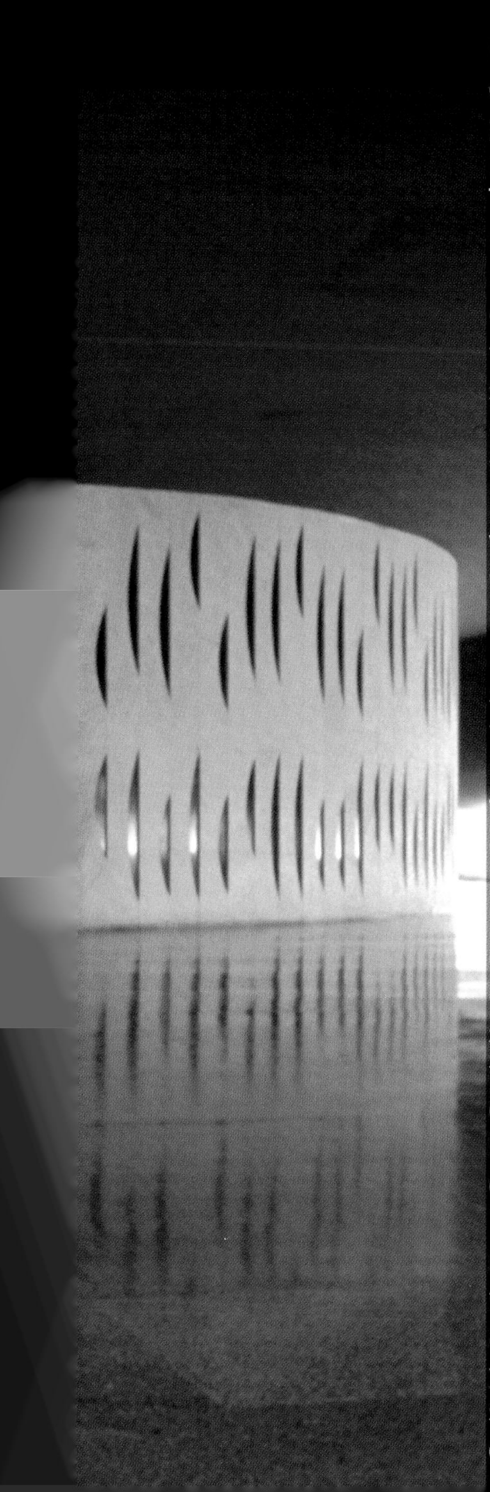

of the chronocratic basis of this plan in which the calculating treatment of time was the main thing. The label 'utopian' is also likely to mislead us if we interpret this as the realization of a long-cherished dream. Here, it is far more a matter of timing – making a burst of speed at the right moment. These considerations take us away from the order of expressions and outcomes, into that of chance and vertigo, which are the main components of the Great Brasilienspiel. It is not the content that counts here, but the move itself. In the middle of the desert of pointlessness, it establishes the term of waiting for the effect. It is a move, whether or not provided with idealistic and utopian forms of expression, of which the hardness of architectural realization makes the founders smile the smile of someone who is initiated in the chronocratic order of surprising and scoring off ones rivals. They know that, past all criticism from the order of sense, they have made a move that reached beyond the point of no return.

The first design Lúcio Costa made for Brasília shows a cross, the second a kite and the third an aircraft. Cross, topographic fixation of the middle; but also intersection, the movement from the pure extremity to the impure centre, and

crucifixion, nailing down. Crossed aeroplane, aeroplane crucified on the cross, crossplane. Thus the symbol of the political kinetic fuses with the cryptological logic of the place. The aeroplane is here in its final resting place: the place of catastrophe, of stranding. And where action congeals, the martyr arises...

One axis, which runs roughly from the west to the east, takes the form of an 8 kilometre long, 400 metre wide esplanade. This monumental grassy plain, where dust and wind have free play and whose dimensions imitate those of the Champs Elysees in Paris, is flanked by the sculptural architecture of Niemeyer. It is this axis which gives Brasília its image, and the architecture sited alongside it provides the logos which have made it world famous. It is the fuselage of the crossplane. The second axis, which is slightly curved and lies roughly north-south, spans the residential function. It takes the form of 14 by 3 kilometre ribbon city which is transected halfway by the monumental axis. The residential ribbon constitutes the wings of the crossplane. The heart of Brasília lies at the intersection of the two axes. It has the form of a box-shaped, three-storey covered shopping centre with a bus terminal beneath it. Each axis is equipped with an ar-

D.A.E.
PLUVIAIS

an artery of multiple carriage ways, giving a total of 14 traffic lanes, which form the empty, smooth surface for motorized traffic. Because the complex multi-level intersections are carried through consistently, the traffic system has a generous roominess.

Brasília's spaciousness makes it incredibly transparent and gives it the Gestalt quality of a TV commercial. Once you have seen it, you will never forget it.

'It has just rained and the air is sultry. The evening sun illumines a dramatic sky. Along the Esplanada dos Ministérios, buildings with facades of green slats stand silhouetted against a purple firmament. Bowls, hemispheres, indefinable curves, boxes and slabs, forms half submerged in the ground, bathe in a remarkable radiance as though on another planet. Everywhere I notice glinting metals, shining stone and pale concrete. Apart from the martial array of the ministries, each separate building along the monumental axis has something of a figure stepping forward out of the background, breaking the bond with its surroundings, a figure whose only aspiration is to set itself off against the overwhelming sky. The atmosphere is elegant and monotonous. Every figure is perfect. The whitish buildings, in which the ex-

pressive breadth of span of the Modern Style is taken to its utmost limit, radiate an indefinable sanctity. In the middle of, or perhaps precisely because of, all this expressive individuality, I detect nonetheless the progress of 'whitewashing', an evening-out of things into monotony, which is compelled by a higher principle. It reminds me of the white masks of a Venetian carnival, or perhaps the sacrificial temples of the Aztecs. The religious quality, which nestles down in between things, is like the crystalline flush of an order that arises from the excessive separation of functions and objects. In contrast to the European city, the distinction between the parts is not caused here by the notching of a body that would otherwise be too full, too large, for comprehension. Here, the gouging has become the emptiness, and the body of the city, in as far as that can be said to exist, altered into a pure distance-making backdrop without specific features, a backdrop that hides in the shadow of negation. Brasília consists of a collection of perfect objects that thank their existence to this substrate of emptiness, a theatrical kind of nothingness from which they appear to have emerged and into which they threaten to sink back. City of refuge, desert city, crypt city. The emptiness

penetrates into the heart of the buildings, and the sun pours in from every side; astonishing the visibility, and endless the miracle that remains concealed. I have a sensation that everything is just past its prime, and that death and decay are only biding their time... Where are the people? Where are the crowds to fill this gigantic emptiness, to rend this silence apart and to impose a human scale on this work of the gods? As I tear along the motorways through the centre at 140 kilometres per hour, I still get the feeling that I am standing still. When the Movimento Sem Terra, 200 strong, pitched its camp on the ruddy plain of the central axis, it virtually swallowed them up. Large parts of the buildings around this emptiness are hidden behind the visible parts or beneath the flat ground, which proves to be no more than a carpet.'

Brasília is totally focussed on its national and international 'aura'. The city's form is almost entirely dedicated to communication. It is intended to give expression to a synthesis which is Brazilian in nature and which rises above the 'everyday mixing'. Of course it is a synthesis of form and function, of the beautiful and the useful, of art and technology; and also of Indians and Negroes, of the baroque and the

poetic, of the modern and the traditional. Brasília is often regarded as a functional city. It may well be so, but it is a city without the ideology of the moderns. Without their pathos. Without that bloody infuriating will to achieve purity and authenticity. Functionalism tries to make function into the only and the true meaning of form. If we take the ideal of functionalism in this sense, Brasília is kitsch – if only because the Baroque has been brought into the equation, let alone the rest. In fact, the city is lost to the cause of functionalism. 'To me, functionalism was a temporary constraint, and once contemporary architecture won the day I rejected it completely', Niemeyer said in 1978. He and Costa did not shrink from introducing, alongside the truth of functionalism, a second truth that contaminated the first with abundant, excessive, decorative elements such as the 'disproportionate dimensions' of public space and the 'pointless' special effects of the architecture. Kitsch recognizes that form has no truth, that it can never be more than one of the most beautiful decorations. The Baroque recognizes that form is a phenomenon without basis and that it can arbitrarily adopt the structure of truth or lies. The logical consequence of this confusion is to go beyond func-

tion and to elevate the effect of the meaner. This is the virulence of the 'Brazilian Style'. But owing to the indeterminacy of that style's alibi (its indifference with respect to truth or falsehood), it leaves open the possibility of an artfully higher bid for meaning.

'Something is not quite right here. Everywhere, you can see that the city is deteriorating. I mean not only visible decay, such as the crumbling marble of the buildings on the Square of the Three Powers (Praça dos Três Poderes), such as the shopping malls near the bus station, one of which changes at night into a veritable red light district complete with striptease clubs, and such as the subsidences in the road surface and the washed-away embankments; but also the invisible decay, which is evident from the new plans to sacrifice the fixed image of the city in order to respond to unanticipated developments. Nowadays, for example, taller buildings are sometimes permitted, and traffic lights have been set up in some places that cast a stain on the idea of the free flow of traffic. But what makes me the most uneasy, is... where are all the people?'

When we scan the plateau that lies before us from the somewhat raised white plain of the Square of the Three Powers, we see, roughly

speaking, emptiness. At first sight the city seems to be an island in the wasteland. But as long ago as 1965, the periphery of Brasília was more densely built than the centre. In 1975, Plano Piloto, meant for 700,000 people, had a population of 244,647. In 1988, Brasilia's Plano Piloto was placed on the UNESCO list of world heritage sites. This meant more or less a declaration of death for the centre of the city in urban planning and economic respects, for no buildings may be added that are not in the original design drawings. New economic developments can now no longer be supported by raising the density of offices and homes. So the district will never be allowed to house a population of more than 700,000.

Eleven legitimate satellite towns, including Guará 1, Guará 2, Taguatinga, Samambaia and Ceilândia, plus countless favelas have developed from miserable hovels for the building workers into substantial Brazilian cities. Invisible at a distance of some tens of kilometres, they support a population of 1.6 million souls – 85 percent of the population of Greater Brasília. Neither in physical nor in social and economic respects do the satellite towns show the least resemblance to the model city. They lack a symbolic urban form. Apart from the fa-

velas, which have much more complex forms, they were laid out as grid cities in the form of building plots fringing a road at the same time as the Plano Piloto. The government then provided water supply points and electricity, followed by water mains, sewers and street paving, and, finally, administration. The satellite cities house mainly people from the direct vicinity and from North-East Brazil, and they survive on the local economy. These are the people who uphold the generosity of space in Brasília. With as many people as possible together in as small as possible an area, they squander space... so as to protect the grandeur of emptiness elsewhere.

Taguatinga, Ceilândia, Samambaia. Here the common people have a right to exists: noise, small shops, buses, hustle and bustle... an untidy clutter. The bus wheels splash mud from the road roughly and indiscriminately in all directions. With a hiss, the front doors open, and we try cheerfully to record the human misery on video and in photographs. The smiling child beams at us with opulence, the promise of the under-developed, the not yet. Plano Piloto, around six in the evening. Vehicles are flooding out of the city. Long queues wait at the bus stops. Despite the spatial separation,

it is the traffic engineering, the numbers and the local economy that give the satellite towns their vitality of precluded rest, a rest that permanently threatens to absorb the exclusive model.

If we reason in terms not of the region but of communicative space, Brasília is not an island at all. It has been closely tied into the global air transport network from the start. For the air-travelling elite, the city degrades into a suffocating place of incarceration and an exchangeable theatre-in-the-round. For this reason alone, Brasília the monument has become a worthless memory as far as the humanistic idea is concerned. The state officials/inhabitants jump in and out of their planes. Anyone who works and anyone who can goes by air. Many people abandon the city every weekend. As a transit city of baroque dimensions, Brasília becomes an apparition inhabited by shades, a kind of anamorphosis of the threshold on which there falls the shadow of the last remnants of the abode that once formed the basis of the city and the urban culture.

At ground level, the flying culture repels the land culture. At the interurban bus station of Brasília, by the 'gateways' of Plano Piloto, the buses of the Ministry of Social Affairs stand waiting every day ready

HISTÓRIA do BRASIL
LITERATURA
TELEBRAS

to ship the stream of candidate residents – the attraction of Brasília is not without success – directly to one of the satellite towns. This division over two types of space makes the city a model for the rise of all those other closed forms and city zones that sunder themselves from their surroundings and go to make up the scattered universe of the non-continent of speed.

Beyond suspense, the Apocalypse of Brasília will be bipartite. On the one hand it falls prey to the voracious absorptive capacity of the living masses, and on the other hand it is enchanted by the syncretism of the signs.

It is easy to see from the air that Greater Brasília has the shape of a ribbon city that runs from south to north, where it makes a gentle bend eastwards and terminates in Plano Pilato. It consist of French-style banlieus with urban-villa like apartments, Asiatic urban fragments in the form of closely-packed nondescript four-storey buildings smothered with advertisements, South American fragments with stuccoed two-storey patio houses, grid-pattern favelas with red-brick slums, and tent villages with much plastic sheeting. The crossplane turns its back on all this and looks away from it. Supported by the urban planning of recent decades, this

conglomeration is veined with excellent roads that allow the traffic to reach every part. That is exactly what you experience in the evening in Brasília – an absurdly heavy traffic load that can only come from outside. If we now half close our eyes, we can see how the conglomeration takes the shape of a slightly bent caboclo, vibrating in its place, with an annoying fly on its nose.

The Brazilians tend to undermine official meanings by fusing two equal components – by syncretism. The Candomblé religion subordinates African demons to Catholic saints. Its adherents thus experience Catholicism in the double light of multiple meanings. The figure of the Virgin Mary is for example syncretized with that of Yemanjá, the African goddess of water. Who can say what is going on in the mind of the devotee who kneels praying before a statue of the Virgin, while in the grip of the African spectre concealed within Her? In the same way as the Brazilian cause was subordinated to Functionalism and Modernism, the Brazilian people slip their own (possibly subversive) meaning under every official meaning, with an evident predilection for maximum intensity and always going one better.

Brasília is thus the symbol of a

movement that wants the city to fulfil once more its task and duty as a capital and a city of the future. It tries to outdo the reality of Brasília as a relic of Modernism by pinning hope to a higher dimension. Modern air-travel culture is trumped by angels, gods, demons and the stars. Under their guiding light, Brasília will become the capital of the Third Millennium. Even emptier than the desert scrublands are the universe, the heavens, the endless vastness of the cosmos and the invisible. What is stronger than the rational utopias of the twentieth century? The irrational expectations of the twenty-first. What is more surprising that the logical outcome of linear progress, or all the great works of human will? It is revelation, or all that reaches out to us from the other side and will rescue us. And what travels faster than a plane? The UFO, the alien, the incarnation of a divinity. From the radical emptiness of the future and the cosmos, a sign will be given, and it will be given in the place that is most ready for it: Brasília. This sign will usher in the finale of Brasília. In Brasília, the races will finally, irrevocably blend. Thanks to this fusion, and not until it has taken place, Brasília will become the true capital of Brazil.

popu
9.62

1. São Paulo is a world city and Brazil is its hinterland.

2. Like a huge, dynamic mass of gridded patches and structureless emulsions of masonry, asphalt, cars and people, the colossus sprawls across the endless plateau and gobbles its way through the dark green forest, leaving little reddish spots behind. The new developments and the mutations follow the logic of land speculation and are driven by instantaneous impulses such as a randomly placed new factory or an equally randomly placed favela. Admittedly, the ring of motorways around and through the centre, together with the railways and two rivers, form a bundle of infrastructure that allows us a distant panorama, and the built-up area occasionally follows an undulation of the landscape, but ultimately these nuances vanish amid the hugeness and chaos of the whole. Thus São Paulo has the appearance of a vast, monotonous, dense uplift cut across by deep clefts.

3. São Paulo occupies an area of 8051 square kilometres. Of this, 1771 square kilometres is built up. The city lies at an elevation of 860 metres.

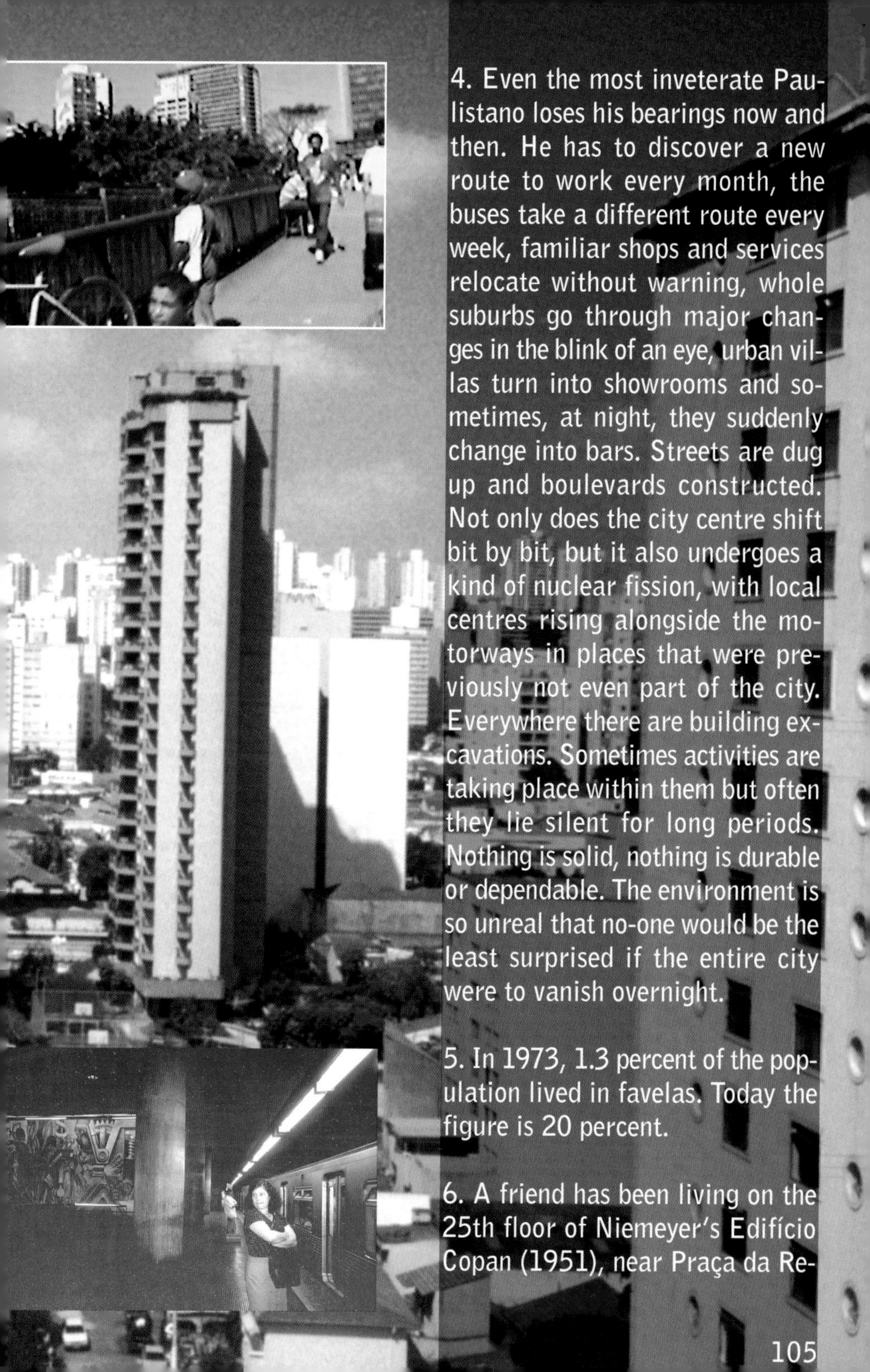

4. Even the most inveterate Paulistano loses his bearings now and then. He has to discover a new route to work every month, the buses take a different route every week, familiar shops and services relocate without warning, whole suburbs go through major changes in the blink of an eye, urban villas turn into showrooms and sometimes, at night, they suddenly change into bars. Streets are dug up and boulevards constructed. Not only does the city centre shift bit by bit, but it also undergoes a kind of nuclear fission, with local centres rising alongside the motorways in places that were previously not even part of the city. Everywhere there are building excavations. Sometimes activities are taking place within them but often they lie silent for long periods. Nothing is solid, nothing is durable or dependable. The environment is so unreal that no-one would be the least surprised if the entire city were to vanish overnight.

5. In 1973, 1.3 percent of the population lived in favelas. Today the figure is 20 percent.

6. A friend has been living on the 25th floor of Niemeyer's Edifício Copan (1951), near Praça da Re-

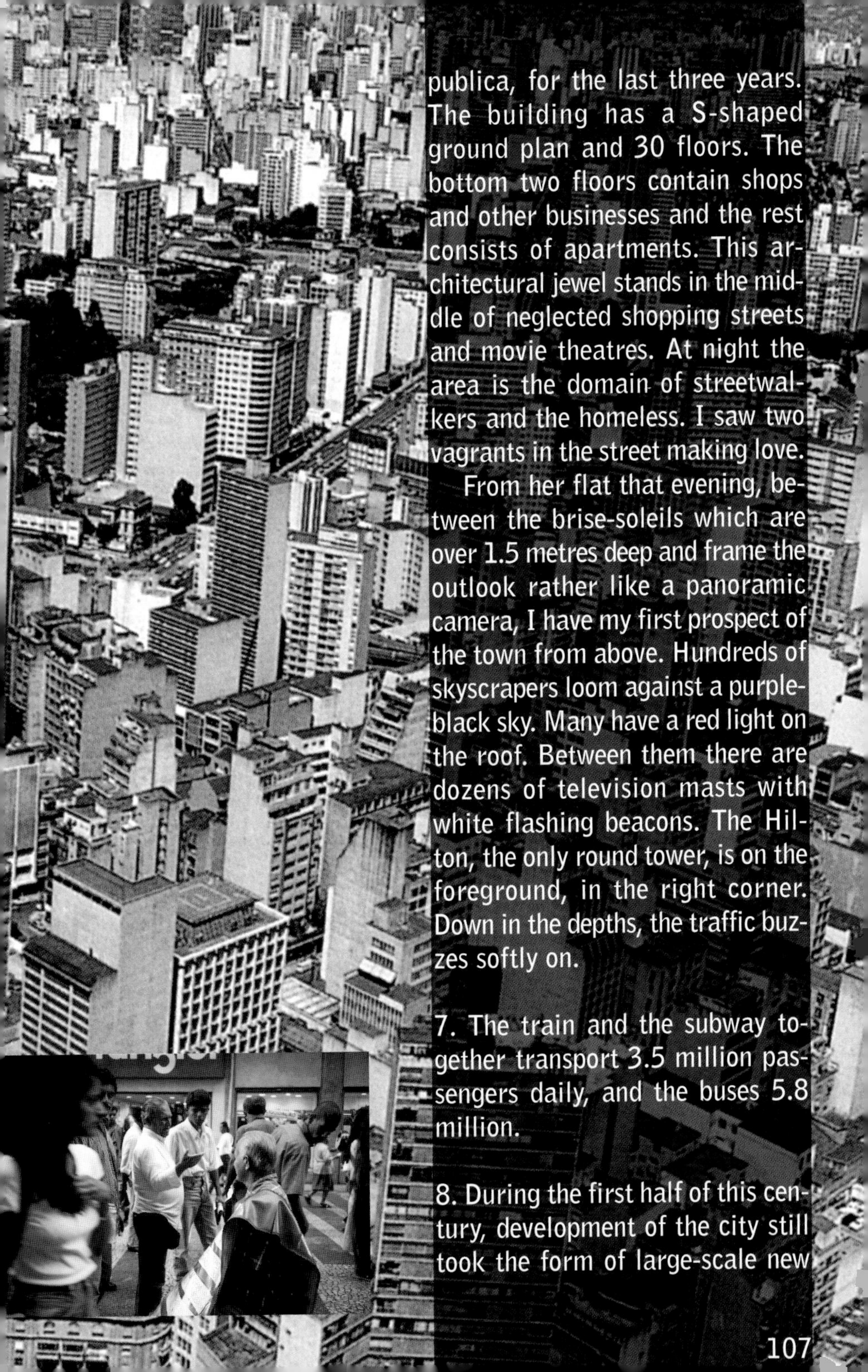

publica, for the last three years. The building has a S-shaped ground plan and 30 floors. The bottom two floors contain shops and other businesses and the rest consists of apartments. This architectural jewel stands in the middle of neglected shopping streets and movie theatres. At night the area is the domain of streetwalkers and the homeless. I saw two vagrants in the street making love.

From her flat that evening, between the brise-soleils which are over 1.5 metres deep and frame the outlook rather like a panoramic camera, I have my first prospect of the town from above. Hundreds of skyscrapers loom against a purple-black sky. Many have a red light on the roof. Between them there are dozens of television masts with white flashing beacons. The Hilton, the only round tower, is on the foreground, in the right corner. Down in the depths, the traffic buzzes softly on.

7. The train and the subway together transport 3.5 million passengers daily, and the buses 5.8 million.

8. During the first half of this century, development of the city still took the form of large-scale new

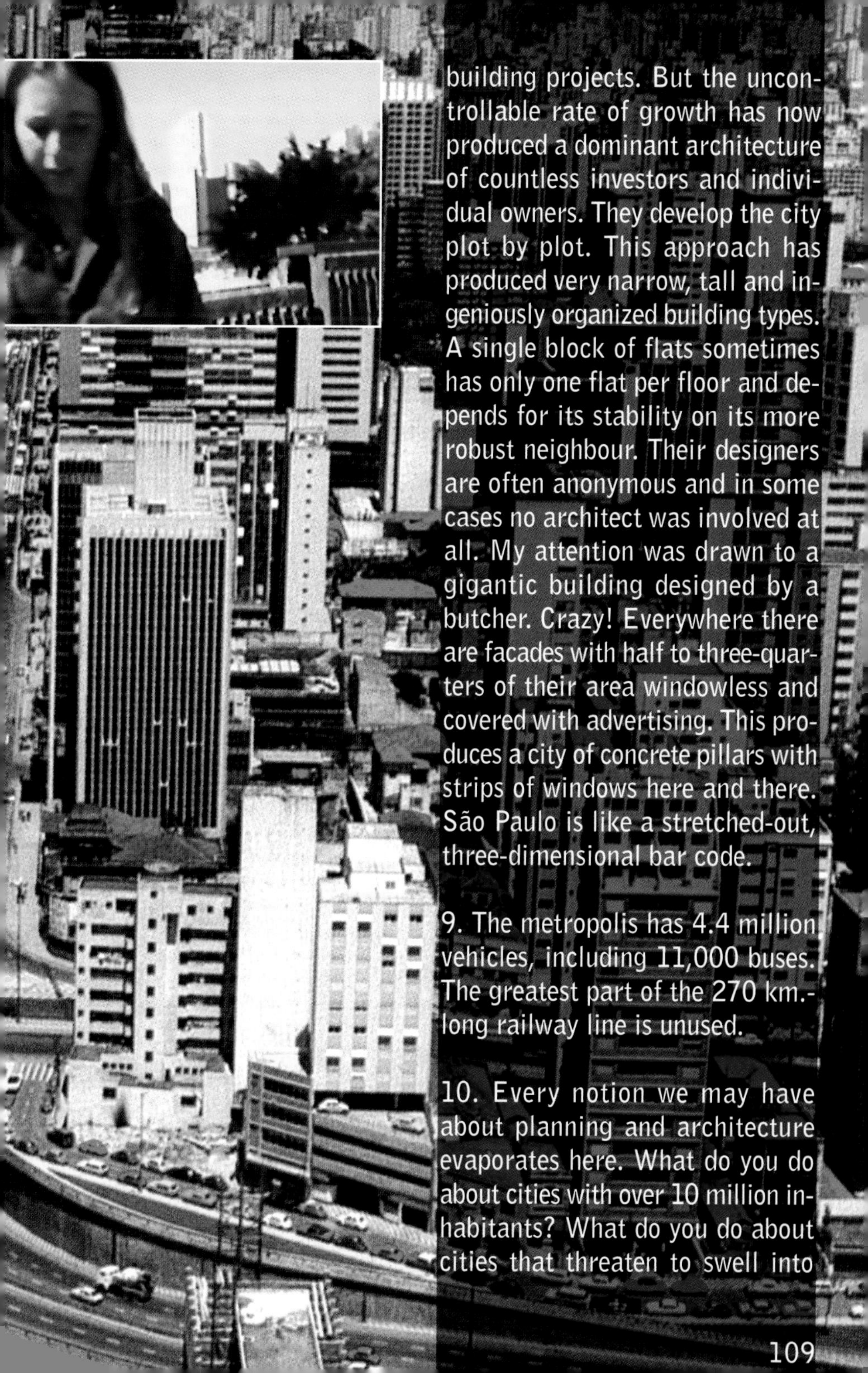

building projects. But the uncontrollable rate of growth has now produced a dominant architecture of countless investors and individual owners. They develop the city plot by plot. This approach has produced very narrow, tall and ingeniously organized building types. A single block of flats sometimes has only one flat per floor and depends for its stability on its more robust neighbour. Their designers are often anonymous and in some cases no architect was involved at all. My attention was drawn to a gigantic building designed by a butcher. Crazy! Everywhere there are facades with half to three-quarters of their area windowless and covered with advertising. This produces a city of concrete pillars with strips of windows here and there. São Paulo is like a stretched-out, three-dimensional bar code.

9. The metropolis has 4.4 million vehicles, including 11,000 buses. The greatest part of the 270 km.-long railway line is unused.

10. Every notion we may have about planning and architecture evaporates here. What do you do about cities with over 10 million inhabitants? What do you do about cities that threaten to swell into

metropolises of 25 million inhabitants (São Paulo, Rio de Janeiro)? What do you do about cities that were planned for a few hundred thousand people but within a few decades have 2 to 3 million inhabitants (Brasília, Belo Horizonte)? You cannot do them justice with 'normal' planning or 'normal' architecture. That would suggest that the contemplative slowness of the plan or design would work here. In Brazil, action is chronically overtaken by events. No time for consideration, no time for reflection. That's a European luxury, but here every municipal organization is powerless against the proliferation of the city. All that can be done is to keep things under control. Urban planning becomes a matter of policing rather than a political or cultural discipline.

11. In a street near the ring road, the Marginais, an architect has spent years developing and building little towers in various architectural styles.

12. The favela may be seen as a 'strategic' land reservation. Where there is a favela, the land prices remain low, even though the location is often close to important urban and regional routes. Pro-

perty developers are able to clear the settlement at a certain point and set down a new industrial zone, office park or housing estate with relative ease and, owing to the cheap land, at low expense. Thus in São Paulo, the favela heads a series of urban functions that follow one after another in the same location. The favela is necessary to the development of the city because it guarantees that land can be freed quickly. Changes in the form and function of a certain area always begin with the favela, which thus provides the fixed framework which gives a place to the series of events of which São Paulo consists.

13. From 1987 to 1991, the city had an average of 1,312,107 housing units, 239,504 hospital beds and 18,544 doctors.

14. Meeting houses of the Candomblé, known as terreiros, were usually located in the poorer districts. The religion is now no longer restricted to the poor and the Negroes, and these houses may now be anywhere, including in wealthier districts such as Pinheiros, Vila Mariana and the Jardins, in the vicinity of subway stations and in ethnic neighbourhoods such

as the predominantly Japanese Liberdade and Jewish Bom Retiro.

Many terreiros have insufficient space. In the terreiro of Minas de Thoya Jarina, the ritual has therefore been modified: in Father Francelino's living room, which measures only four square metres in area, now some twenty adherents can dance and sway in honour of the gods. Candomblé, which is supposed to take place in the purely natural surroundings, does not belong in a city. But the magic imagination will not be suppressed by cramped conditions and logic, and it banks on the multi-dimensionality of the metropolis.

15. The population grew at a rate of 3 percent per annum for a long time, but now it is growing only with 0.5 percent.

16. The din of the traffic indicates the adrenalin-level of São Paulo. Power City. It roars in the morning, it roars at night, it roars the whole day long. The city is one huge engine. The engine of Brazil. Nor is it shy about the fact. Naturally there are places where the noise is subdued, such as in a few parks and residential areas, but then they are really oases in a city that has not been laid out under normal

conditions but has been ground o
of the earth by an incessant strea
of vehicles. Just as the water of
river can create a canyon, the tra
fic of São Paulo has made it
streets.

If someone were to ask me what I am doing here in Brazil, I can only reply that I am mentally straying, tanning my brains or getting permanently rid of a few obstinate prejudices and automatisms. And why not in Brazil?

17. It is freedom and expansion that matter in São Paulo, not historical continuity.

18. The Paulistanos do not see their city as a landscape, for they have no aesthetic bond with it. They either live in the thick of it and are barely distinguishable from it, or do distinguish themselves from it and experience it as inimical neo-nature. For those immersed in São Paulo, the surroundings resemble a universe of temptations and metamorphoses, where large areas of the city take on human traits and where people come to resemble the city. As neo-nature, the city is respectively resistance, future, adventure, obligation and... an absurd secret.

Since the city demands so much

energy from its inhabitants, from their intuition and emotions, not enough remains to apply to one's fellow citizen, for example to improve him. The inclination to manipulate and educate is strange to the Paulistano. If there is solidarity here, it is not impelled by a sense of responsibility but by a conspiracy against the metropolis.

19. Machismo and feminismo: except for the banks, Brazil is ruled by women.

20. In Grande Sertão: Veredas (The Devil to Pay in the Backlands, 1963), Guimarães Rosa wrote that the Brazilian interior was undeveloped, but it did have culture. Other forces, chiefly magic ones, predominated there. If the culture of the interior were integrated with that of the cities, a new Brazilian man would arise. Euclides Da Cunha had earlier related in Os Sertões (Rebellion in the Backlands, 1902/1947) how an occult-messianic revolt had been beaten down by a 'cold-hearted, technical-functional' army. Brazilians, he argued, had a duty to colonize the interior and so blend the occult-messianic and the technical-functional facets of their culture.

Today's São Paulo has a cul-

TÁ NERVOSO?
ENTÃO FIQUE.
EDDIE MURPHY

tural mix containing not only Negro magic and Indian ritual but Shintoism, Zen, Tai Chi, French Positivism, a bit of German Idealism, a pinch of American Pragmatism, Neapolitan music, North Italian Futurism, Russian Orthodoxy, Dutch Calvinism, Spanish Mysticism and Jewish Intellectualism.

21. Mario de Andrade's Macunaíma (1928) depicts a spineless hero and fantasizes about people who know no responsibility.

22. The new man lives on fashion. He thus liberates himself from the obligation to authenticity. His great passion is to apply information, models, strategies and all kinds of examples from elsewhere to his daily life, and to turn them into reality. In so doing he can experience the finest of what someone else has already experienced. In philosophy and literature, this results in the lightness of dilettantism, an intellectual delight in anything that is new, and that brings into being such marvellous fusions as magic positivism, spiritualistic logical analysis, Marxist kaballa and Zen Catholicism. By the way, the basis for this fashion-following and dilettantism is always the new

6435
6435 10
27 385
31 816

man's abysmal openness to seduction. At the end of all this mixing together, two things rise to the surface – the genius of the feminine, and liberation from prejudice.

23. São Paulo, hotel. Milton Vargas said, 'The Brazilians are not convinced that they live in reality'.

24. They are apparently unfamiliar with the idea of team spirit here. You can see from their football that they do not know how to deploy themselves. Twenty of them at a time run after the ball, without strategy, and it depends solely on the qualities of the individual player who will ultimately win. They are incapable of creating openings, of making room for a team-mate to improve his position. This is moreover an impression you get in Brazil as a whole. Their personal space is far to cramped, both physically and mentally.

But isn't team spirit much too European a notion? Suppose it's not at all the group as a whole that matters, but solely the excellence of the individual. Perhaps that's precisely the power of a system that is the very opposite of self-organization. As a group they are a mess, but as a synergy of talented individuals the Brazilians

Meat Grill
TELESP
RS 17,90 BOLO
INTEIRO
PROMOÇAo
TAXI

will undoubtedly come out on top.

25. Brazil has an area of 850 million hectares. 70% of the land is privately owned. Of the landowners, 3% own less than 10 ha. 35% own more than 1,000 ha. 28% own more than 10,000 ha. 42% of the large landholdings are nonproductive.

26. Something happens in my heart / every time I cross Ipiranga and Avenida São João / when I first came here, I understood nothing / neither the hard, concrete poetry of your street corners / nor the discrete inelegance of your women / when I gazed at you / I did not see my own face / I called what I saw poor taste / the poor taste of poor taste! / for Narcissus finds everything ugly that is not a reflection / you gave me a difficult start / what I do not know from afar, / from a different, happy dream of the city / quickly teaches to call you 'reality' / because you are the opposite of the opposite of the opposite of the opposite.

27. Belo Horizonte. The eternally repudiated city. Brasília. The eternally unfinished city. Rio de Janeiro. The eternally dreaming city. São Paulo. The city that

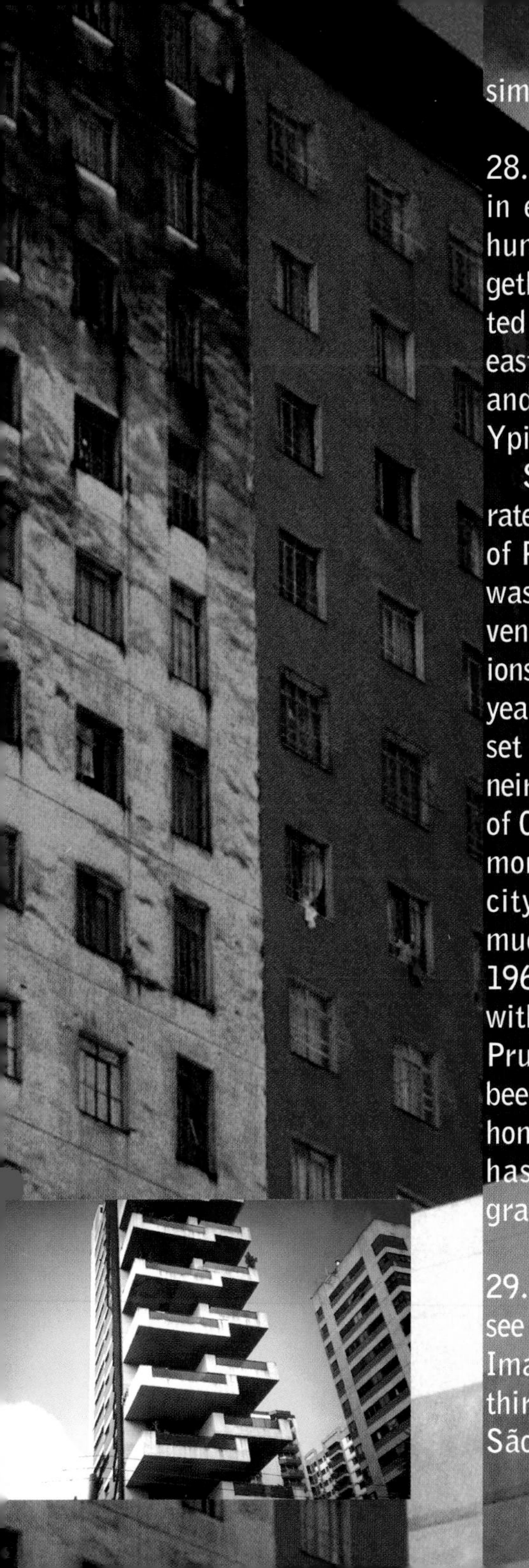

simply roars.

28. In the favela of Vila Prudente in eastern São Paulo, over five hundred people are packed together in the blue and green painted 'salon'. Music from the north-eastern region is playing, as usual, and the customers are drinking Ypioca sugar cane whiskey.

Severino José da Silva, illiterate, left Itora in the interior region of Pernambuco in 1948, when he was sixteen. He became a street vendor of potatoes, garlic and onions in the city centre of Recife. Ten years later, he had saved enough to set off on a freighter to Rio de Janeiro to join his family in the favela of Caxias. After a further eighteen months, he moved to São Paulo, a city about which he had heard much. Severino arrived there in 1960 and immediately went to stay with a cousin in the favela of Vila Prudente. Since then, he has never been back to Rio de Janeiro or his home town. He married, and now has five children and three grandchildren.

29. A city without a horizon. You see skyscrapers wherever you look. Imagine Manhattan multiplied by thirty and you get something like São Paulo.

2º ANDAR
1º ANDAR
LONDON CALLING
Zoyd
RUA ALTA

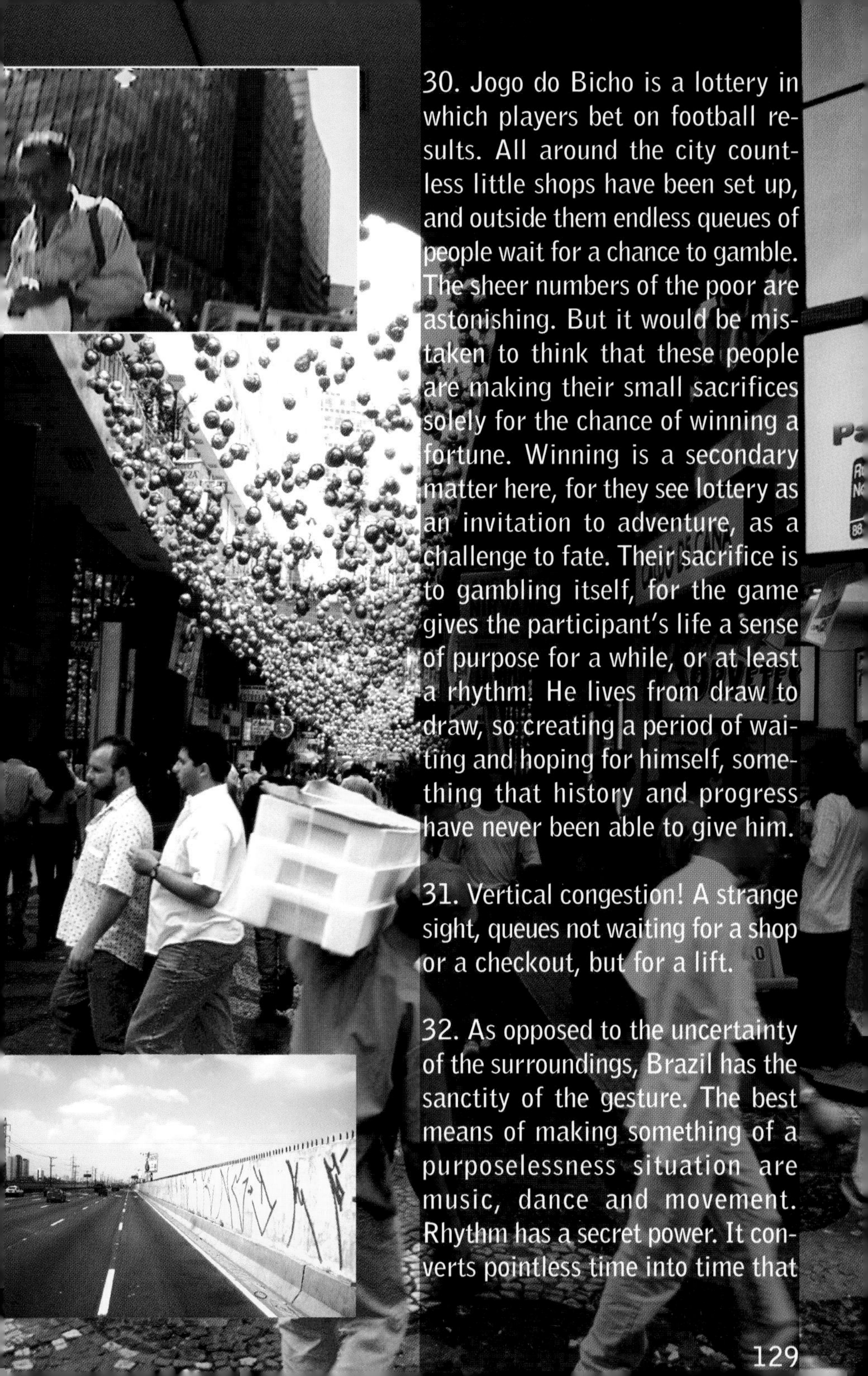

30. Jogo do Bicho is a lottery in which players bet on football results. All around the city countless little shops have been set up, and outside them endless queues of people wait for a chance to gamble. The sheer numbers of the poor are astonishing. But it would be mistaken to think that these people are making their small sacrifices solely for the chance of winning a fortune. Winning is a secondary matter here, for they see lottery as an invitation to adventure, as a challenge to fate. Their sacrifice is to gambling itself, for the game gives the participant's life a sense of purpose for a while, or at least a rhythm. He lives from draw to draw, so creating a period of waiting and hoping for himself, something that history and progress have never been able to give him.

31. Vertical congestion! A strange sight, queues not waiting for a shop or a checkout, but for a lift.

32. As opposed to the uncertainty of the surroundings, Brazil has the sanctity of the gesture. The best means of making something of a purposelessness situation are music, dance and movement. Rhythm has a secret power. It converts pointless time into time that

has some point. Rhythm has the power to structure the movements of daily life and give them an added aesthetic, ritual and sacral dimension. The boy's dancing gait, the private smile, the rattling of the typewriter as though it were a tom-tom, licking an envelope behind the post-office counter, starting a video recorder, opening the door. Every gesture, even the gesture of fighting, has a certain cultivated quality here. Amid a sea of purposelessness there thus rises the sacrosanctity of the gesture, in which is celebrated the supremacy of the body, with its undulations, its sensuality and its expressiveness.

33. Macumba – turn the mind into a body. Umbanda.

34. Despite the impotence of the authorities, Brazil is not unplanned. That is a myth. Worship of the cheerful Brazilian chaos is typically European. Everything is planned here, as it is in Western Europe. Perhaps the layout is less well-structured and less successful, but once you abandon the idea that space has to be the medium or the mirror of a certain order and accept that time is the crucial factor here, the Brazilian sense of order suddenly discloses itself every-

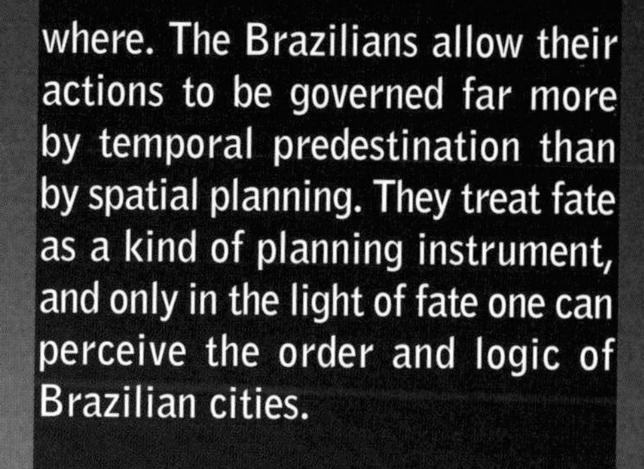

where. The Brazilians allow their actions to be governed far more by temporal predestination than by spatial planning. They treat fate as a kind of planning instrument, and only in the light of fate one can perceive the order and logic of Brazilian cities.

35. Anhangabaú, Pindamonhangaba. Do not speak in sentences but in semantic blocks of fused verbal roots. He who speaks thus, wards off the curse of development.

36. In a shop, one assistant is required to fetch my order from the shelves. A second assistant, on another counter, packs the little box in paper. At the next counter, elsewhere in the shop, I pay a third shop assistant for the purchase and get my change. All this takes place at such a lethargic rate that my sense of effectiveness is undermined. I have wondered a thousand times about the true significance of this nationally nurtured slow-motion. Is it a sign of poverty or of superiority? Probably the latter. Brazilians spread all actions out in time, and take the time to dissolve time in dilated action.

37. Furia da figura. Believe in nothing but style.

CAPTIONS

RIO DE JANEIRO

Cover: This model of telephone was popularly dubbed the orelhão, or 'big ear'. They may be found all over the city. They are still doing good service even on the sands of Ipanema. Brazilians love talking on the phone.

1 Cycle rack on the Praia de Copacabana. In the distance, built against the rocks, Forte de Copacabana.

2/3 Praia de Joá, with the Pão de Açúcar (Sugar Loaf) in the background.

4/5 Praia do Ingá, with the Museu de Arte Contemporânea(MAC) in the background.

5a Antônio in an alley in Favela Ladeira dos Funcionários.

6/7 Standard product of Brazilian pavers at Copacabana.

6a Aerial view of the favelas in the hills of Rio de Janeiro.

7a Alley in Favela Ladeira dos Funcionários.

8 Red Mucuna Bennettii, Burle Marx collection, Sítio Santo Antônio da Bica in Pedra de Guaratiba, near Rio de Janeiro.

8a Residents' indoor garage in an apartment flat, Ipanema.

9 Artocarpus Integra, originally from Asia, flourishing in Brazil. It has a penetrating scent and can reach 60 cm. in height.

9a Alley in Favela Ladeira dos Fu cionários.

10/11 Swinging pavement motif

10a The Bay of Guanabara and t sinusoid curve of the Botafogo d trict. The Pão de Açúcar enters in a play of contours with Rio's curvi waterfront.

10b Tunel Dois Irmãos connec Zona Zul to Barra da Tijuca.

10c Bay of Rio seen from the Sug Loaf, with Christ Redeemer in t background.

10d Clube Costa Brava in hard-t find Rua Sargento José da Silva, r 3621.

11a Antônio in an alley in Fave Ladeira dos Funcionários.

12/13 Museu de Arte Contempor nea in Niterói, on the far side of t Bay of Guanabara, designed Oscar Niemeyer. The building popularly known as 'Jupiter 5', aft a flying saucer in the North Ame can sci-fi TV series 'Lost in Spac

13a Alley in Favela Ladeira d Funcionários.

14/15 In the glass gondola, a proaching ever closer to the Sug Loaf. The view is dazzling.

14a The Edifício Marques de He val in the city centre of Rio is a f ties classic by the three-man arch tectural team of M.M.M. Rober

14b Walled condomínios in Bar da Tijuca.

14c The apartments in Niterói off a view of Niemeyer's Museu de Ar

ontemporânea.
.4d Condomínios in Barra da
'ijuca.
.5a Girl Nina with dummy in Favela
.adeira dos Funcionários.
.6/17 Pedra da Gávea.
.6a Security guardhouse by the
anco Real.
7a Girl Nina with dummy in Favela
adeira dos Funcionários.
8/19 Copacabana, Ipanema and
rca seen from the Sugar Loaf.
8a Intersection in Ipanema. Part
the Rio-Cidade project. Designed
the architectural firm of Paulo
asé.
9a Girl Nina with dummy in Favela
adeira dos Funcionários.
0/21 Copacabana, view of traffic
nes, the beach, pavements, foot-
aths, greenery and mosaic pave-
ent motifs, designed by Roberto
urle Marx in the seventies.
0a The 'mountain village', Favela
Roçinha, is the largest urban
um in the world with a popula-
on of 300 thousand.
.a Nina's little sister in the Favela
adeira dos Funcionários.
2/23 Tunel Dois Irmãos, the sp-
ndid double-deck route that con-
cts Ipanema and Leblon to Barra
Tijuca. You drive from the city to
rra on the upper deck and re-
n on the lower deck.
.a Picture of the top part of the
vela da Roçinha.

Ladeira dos Funcionários.
24/25 Corcovado, 709 metres high, where Christ Redeemer greets the city with open arms.
24a Entrances to the dwellings in Favela da Roçinha.
25a Nina's little sister in the Favela Ladeira dos Funcionários.
26 Orchid, Catleya Hybrida, Burle Marx collection, Sítio Santo Antônio da Bica.
26a Youths doing a Capoeira dance in Favela da Roçinha.
27 Evocative rock garden by landscape architect Burle Marx, Fazenda Vargem Grande in the upper state of São Paulo.
27a Nina's little sister in the Favela Ladeira dos Funcionários.
28/29 The world-renowned, five-kilometre long boulevard in Copacabana, constructed in black and white basalt, designed by Burle Marx.
28a Like 'glaciers on the mountainside'. Favela da Roçinha seen from a distance.
29a Nina's little sister in the Favela Ladeira dos Funcionários, en face.
30/31 Sculptural treatment of swimming pool side, with peepholes, in Clube Costa Brava.
30a Drapers' shop in 'Saara', the textile street in the centre of Rio de Janeiro.
30b Drapers' shop in 'Saara', the textile street in the centre of Rio de

30c Drapers' shop in 'Saara', the textile street in the centre of Rio de Janeiro.
30d Drapers' shop in 'Saara', the textile street in the centre of Rio de Janeiro.
31a Antônio playing with Pedro in Favela Ladeira dos Funcionários.
32 Heliconia Rostrata, Burle Marx collection, Sítio Santo Antônio da Bica.
32a Very steep slope in Favela da Roçinha.
33 Aboveground electricity and telephone cables in Favela da Roçinha.
33a Antônio playing with Pedro in Favela Ladeira dos Funcionários.
34/35 A substantial gateway allows entrance to a 'supermarket' for semi-precious stones in Barra da Tijuca. The picture shows one of several one-metre tall 'forests' of amethyst.
34a Greenhouse, Burle Marx collection, Sítio Santo Antônio da Bica.
35a Antônio playing with Pedro in Favela Ladeira dos Funcionários.
36/37 Plants in the street scene: Bismarckia Nobilis.
36a Interior of Museu de Arte Contemporânea, with view of Bay of Guanabara.
36b Entrance to an indoor car park on Avenida Presidente Vargas, in the financial heart of Rio.
36c View of Catedral de São Sebrás in the city centre.
36d. Spread in model house, Favela Ladeira dos Funcionários.

BELO HORIZONTE

38/39 On the fifteenth floor of the Othon Palace Hotel, the combinec noise of passing planes, pneumatic drills and the two million inhabitants of Belo Horizonte besets the traveller.
38a Former Iate Tennis Club ir Pampulha designed by Oscar Niemeyer, a classic dating from 1942
40/41 Climber-covered fence between properties sculptured wit rectangular motifs.
40a Clube Libanês de Belo Horizonte, 1952, on the corner of Avenida Antônio Carlos and Avenid Santa Rosa.
41a Smiling Carolinas in Avenid Afonso Pena.
42 Twin towers. The facade carrie a number of Indian heads in Marajoara style. One of Belo Horizonte' first buildings in this genre.
43 View of the urban grid from th 24th floor of the Othon Palac Hotel.
43a Passers-by in Avenida Afons Pena.
44/45 Orthogonal motif of stacke tins.
45a The back of a waiting woma on Avenida Afonso Pena.

de Janeiro.
Cynar advertisement.
Maria das Dores in Avenida
nso Pena.
49 Orthogonal pattern of flo-
s in a flower-stall in Rua Rio
aneiro.
Bethania (with spectacles) and
élia (in jeans) in Avenida Afonso
a.
Rua da Bahia.
Sitting woman in striped trou-
.
Praça Afonso Arinos, in the
tre.
Bethania (with spectacles) in
nida Afonso Pena.
53 Sculptural transparent screen
he international bank on the
th-west side of Avenida Afonso
a.
a Banana stall on Avenida do
torno.
a Odete and Maria hurrying by on
enida Afonso Pena.
/55 Avenida Bias Fortes, view of
of the diagonal avenues in the
tre.
a Corner of Avenida Afonso Pena
d 7 de Setembro.
/57 Garden of the former Iate
nis Club.
a Litter bins at the Igreja de São
ncisco de Assis in Pampulha.
a Woman waiting at bus-stop on
enida Amazonas.
Tall and short side-by-side on

58a Mobile Police in Avenida Amazonas.
59 Rua da Bahia.
59a Girls waiting at bus-stop on Avenida Amazonas.
60/61 Damaged facade on Avenida Amazonas.
60a Watch house of security service.
61a Passer-by in Avenida Amazonas.
62/63 Rua da Bahia, northward view from the vicinity of Praça da Estaçao.
63a Our female guide in Avenida Amazonas.
64/65 Portrait of a man with a necklace.
65a Our female guide in Avenida Amazonas.
66 Banco do Estado de Minas Gerais, Praça 7 de Setembro.
67 Intersection with painted facades on Avenida Alvares Cabral.
67a Onto the top of the hill, facing the Praça da Liberdade, lays the Edifício Niemeyer: an undulating qualification of a triangular site.
68/69 South facade of Edifício Niemeyer.
68a Pool chairs in the former Iate Tennis Club.

BRASÍLIA

70/71 Monumental axis seen from the Torre de Rádio e Televisão. Both are creations of Lúcio Costa. The

meyer.

70a Street view between two shopping malls, Conjunto Nacional and Conic.

72/73 Memorial JK contains the mortal remains and attributes of President Juscelino Kubitchek, who commissioned the building of Brasília.

72a The enormous empty space in the central axis of Brasília, with the building of the Teatro Nacional in the background.

72b Maria da Aparecida at the Torre de Rádio e Televisão.

74/75 Parliament Building, the visual terminus of the monumental axis.

74a Street view between two shopping malls, Conjunto Nacional and Conic.

76/77 The mortal remains of President Juscelino Kubitchek are preserved behind this artistic relief.

76a Red earth and skating children in Samambaia.

78/79 Under the spectacular skies of Brasília, the conference centre by architect Sérgio Bernardes. The elongated building had an immense white canvas fastened to the guys. The canvas flew off on the first 'desert storm' and landed three federal states away.

78a João at the Torre de Rádio e Televisão.

78b Street view between two shopping malls, Conjunto Nacional and Conic.

79a Spacious interior of the Co
junto Nacional shopping mall.

79b Conjunto Nacional is the fir
shopping mall in the 'heart'
Brasília. It acts as a beacon, a m
niature Las Vegas, in this city
civil servants.

80/81 Flamboyant staircase in th
Ministry of Foreign Affairs, th
Palácio do Itamaraty.

80a Brasília manhole cover.

82 Torre de Rádio e Televisão give
a view of the whole Plano Piloto.

82a Street view between two shop
ping malls, Conjunto Nacional an
Conic.

83 Praça dos Três Poderes, with
view of the Panteão da Pátri
through the veranda of the Suprem
Tribunal Federal, both designed b
Oscar Niemeyer.

83a The Panteão da Pátria, dusk

84/85 Lobby in the Congresso Na
cional.

84a Gabriel at the Torre de Rádi
e Televisão.

84b Seating area in the grass c
the central reservation.

86/87 Greenery on the roof of th
Congresso Nacional.

86a Street view between two shop
ping malls, Conjunto Nacional an
Conic.

87a Atmospheric illuminations
Praça dos Três Poderes.

88/89 The annexes of the ministr
buildings with sunblinds.

88a Bus stop, Esplanada dos Ministérios.
90/91 Congresso Nacional, view of ramp and main towers.
90a Gabriel at the Torre de Rádio e Televisão.
90b Street view between two shopping malls, Conjunto Nacional and Conic.
92/93 Monumental staircase leading to Supremo Tribunal Federal.
92a Clara and Clotilda.
93a João and Pedro.
94/95 Public space, Samambaia.
94a Street view between two shopping malls, Conjunto Nacional and Conic.
95a Tourists before the Presidential Palace.
96/97 Concrete bus shelter
96a Waldir at the Torre de Rádio e Televisão.
97a View of Setor Hoteleiro Sul.
97b Lying opposite the Ministry of Defence, the Quartel-General do Exército, a fine park designed by Burle Marx.
98/99 Public space, Samambaia.
98a Street view between two shopping malls, Conjunto Nacional and Conic.
99a Elegant staircase in the Ministry of Foreign Affairs, the Palácio do Itamaraty.
99b Multi-level intersections in the monumental central reservation of Brasília, seen form the roof of Hotel Avorada.
100. Portrait of aviator Joaquim.
101. Portrait of Joãozinho in Samambaia.

SÃO PAULO

102/103 View of São Paulo.
102a Avenida Paulista, westward view.
104/105 View from the sports tower at the SESC Fábrica da Pompéia.
104a Avenida Paulista, eastward view.
105a Two coloured boys on the Viaduto do Chá.
105b Estação da Sé, subway station.
106/107 View from Edifício Itália, with Edifício Copan at left of picture.
107a Living, walking advertising posters.
108/109 View of city boulevard.
108a Tânia Maria in holiday mode, disguised as 'Carioca'.
109a Girl on the Viaduto do Chá.
110/111 The city's central district seen from Edifício Copan, facing south.
110b 'Seu' Pedro Paulo.
112/113 The Minhocão, one of the first major viaducts over the Vale do Anhangabaú.
112a High rise.
113a Fat boy on the Viaduto do Chá.
114 From Edifício Martinelli, Avenida São João/Avenida Libero Ba-

daró (1929), view over the central area between Praça das Bandeiras, Praça da Sé and Praça do Correio, facing south-east towards Praça da Sé.
115 View from Edifício Martinelli, southwards towards Praça das Bandeiras.
116/117 Viaduto do Chá, from Vale do Anhangabaú.
117a Man on the Viaduto do Chá.
117b Safety measures in SESC Fábrica da Pompéia, designed by Lina Bo Bardi, Marcelo Ferraz and André Vainer.
118/119 Street view in the periphery of São Paulo, in the vicinity of Conceição subway station.
118a The Paulista equivalent of the 'Orelhão' on the Viaduto do Chá, in the city centre.
119a Sanitary facilities.
120/121 Facades on Avenida 9 de Julho, in the central area of São Paulo.
121a Man in the Vale do Anhangabaú.
121b Fuel station beneath the road.
122 Viaduct over Vale do Anhangabaú. It forms the link between two sections of the São Paulo city centre.
123 SESC Fábrica da Pompéia, high rise with indoor sports fields, designed by Lina Bo Bardi, Marcelo Ferraz and André Vainer.
123a Rainwater pipe, SESC Fábrica da Pompéia.
124/125 Rua Augusta between Avenida Paulista and Rua Estados Unidos.
124a Sturdy, vandalism-resistant telephone booths.
125a Two coloured men at a bus station in the centre of the city.
125b SESC Fábrica da Pompéia.
126/127 Apartment building on Rua Rodrigues dos Santos, seen form Rua João Teodoro.
127a Apartment building with prominently cantilevered balconies on Rodovia Castello Branco in Alphaville, a gated community outside São Paulo.
128 Interior of a shopping mall in the centre of São Paulo.
129 Shopping street in the Sé district.
129a Tourist in the centre of the city.
129b Endless wall along the Marginais, on the Rio Tietê, seen from São Paulo airport.
130/131 Estação da Sé subway station.
130a Estação da Sé. The intersection of the north-south and east-west subway lines.
131a Group of schoolchildren with their teacher in the Memorial da América Latina.
132/133 Helicopter landing pad on the roof of Edifício Copan.
133a Caucasian woman near the Estação da Sé subway station.
134/135 Prospect of the undula-

ting Brazilian landscape, driving on the Via Anchieta from São Paulo to São José dos Campos.
136/137 View from an unpaved road, somewhere between the small baroque town Aréias and Fazenda Vargem Grande.
138/139 Garden of Fazenda Vargem Grande, designed by the landscape architect Burle Marx.
140/141 Foz do Iguaçú, one of the world's largest waterfalls.
142/143 Some travelling companions in a rubber dinghy, eye to eye with Foz do Iguaçú.
144 Luxuriant garden by Burle Marx, part of the former textile mill Tecelagem Parahyba in São José dos Campos.

TRAVEL SCHEDULE

17.04.97
Amsterdam - Rio de Janeiro
19.04.97
Rio de Janeiro - Brasília
23.04.97
Brasília - Belo Horizonte
25.04.97
Belo Horizonte - São Paulo
29.04.97
São Paulo - Foz do Iguaçú
01.05.97
Foz do Iguaçú - São José dos Campos
02.05.97
São José dos Campos - Aréias
04.05.97
Aréias - Banabal - Rio de Janeiro
11.05.97
Rio de Janeiro - Amsterdam

SITES AND PROJECTS

RIO DE JANEIRO

Aeroporto Santos Dumont (Marcelo and Milton Roberto, gardens of Roberto Burle Marx, 1944)
Avenida Atlântica in Copacabana (Roberto Burle Marx, 1970)
Barra da Tijuca (from 1960)
Bilblioteca Nacional (1905)
Casa das Canoas (Oscar Niemeyer, 1953)
Centro Empresarial Internacional Rio (Edson Musa and Eduardo Musa, 1989)
Clube Costa Brava (Ricardo Menescal and Renarto Menescal, 1962)
Corcovado (1926/1931)
Edifício Avenida Central (Henrique E. Mindlin, 1957)
Edifício Marques do Herval (Marcelo, Milton and Mauricio Roberto, 1952)
Edifício-Sede ABI - Associaçao Brasileira de Imprensa (Marcelo and Milton Roberto, 1936)
Edifício-Sede Petrobrás (Roberto Luiz Gandolfi, José H. Sanchotene, Abraao Assad and Luiz Fortes Netto, 1968)
Favela da Roçinha
Floresta da Tijuca (1861/1874)

Hotel National (Oscar Niemeyer, 1968)
Ipanema Beach
IPLANRIO - Favela Bairro Program, the Caju neighbourhood: Favela Ladeira dos Functionários, Favela Parque São Sebastião
Jardim Botânico Botanic Garden (Roberto Burle Marx, 1949)
Leblon Beach
Museu de Arte Contemporânea, Niterói (Oscar Niemeyer, 1995)
Museu de Arte Moderna (Alfonso Eduardo Reidy, 1953)
Paço Imperial (1743/1985)
Palácio Capanema former Ministry of Education (Le Corbusier a.o., 1937)
Pão de Açúcar Suger Loaf
Parque do Flamengo (Alfonso Eduardo Reidy and Roberto Burle Marx, 1962)
Passarela do Samba (Oscar Niemeyer, 1985)
Praça 15 de Novembro (1889)
Rio Cidade, Urban Renewal, the Penha neighbourhood
São Conrado
Sítio Santo Antônio da Bica (Roberto Burle Marx, 1949)

BELO HORIZONTE

Banco do Estado de Minas Gerais (Oscar Niemeyer, 1953)
Biblioteca Pública Estadual (Oscar Niemeyer, 1954)
Casa do Baile (Oscar Niemeyer, 1942)
Cassino - Museu de Arte Moderne (Oscar Niemeyer, 1942)
Clube Libanês de Belo Horizonte (Moreida, 1952)
Colégio Estadual Minas Gerais (Oscar Niemeyer, 1954)
Conjunto Juscelino Kubitschek (Oscar Niemeyer, 1952)
Edifício Clemente Faria (Alvaro Vital Brazil, 1946)
Edifício Oscar Niemeyer (Oscar Niemeyer, 1951)
Edifício-Sede do BDMG (Humberto Serpa, M. Pinto de Barros, Marcus Vinicius R. Meyer and W.R. Abdalla, 1969)
Iate Tênis Clube (Oscar Niemeyer, 1942)
Igreja São Francisco de Assis (Oscar Niemeyer and Cândido Portinari, 1942)
Parque das Mangabeiras
Parque municipal
Parque da Pampulha (1942)

BRASÍLIA

Catedral Metropolitana Nossa Senhora da Aparecida (Oscar Niemeyer, 1959)
Congresso Nacional (Oscar Niemeyer, 1960/1978)
Espaço Lúcio Costa Space honoured to Lúcio Costa and Oscar Niemeyer (1960)
Esplanada dos Ministérios (Oscar Niemeyer, 1960/1978)

Igreja Nossa Senhora da Fátima (Oscar Niemeyer, 1958)
Memorial Juscelino Kubitchek (Oscar Niemeyer, 1980)
Museu da Cidade (1960)
Palácio da Alvorada e Capela (Oscar Niemeyer, 1958)
Palácio da Justiça Ministry of Justice (Oscar Niemeyer, 1960)
Palácio do Itamaraty Ministry of Foreign Affairs (Oscar Niemeyer and Roberto Burle Marx, 1960)
Palácio do Jaburú (Oscar Niemeyer, Roberto Burle Marx, Alfredo Ceschiatti and M. Perreti, 1958)
Palácio do Planalto Presidential Palace (Oscar Niemeyer, 1960)
Panteão da Pátria Pantheon of the Nation (Oscar Niemeyer, 1960)
Praça dos Três Poderes (1960)
Quartel-general do Exército (Oscar Niemeyer, Milton Ramos and Roberto Burle Marx, 1960)
Rodoviária (Lúcio Costa, 1960)
Setor Bancário Sul (masterplan Oscar Niemeyer, 1975)
Setor Comercial Norte
Setor Residencial - Lago Sul (1960)
Setor Residencial - Super Quadras Quadra 308 Sul (Oscar Niemeyer and Lúcio Costa, 1960)
Supremo Tribunal Federal Supreme Federal Court (Oscar Niemeyer, 1960)
Templo da Legião da Boa Vontade R.R. Roberto, 1989)
Teatro Nacional (Oscar Niemeyer, 1960)
Torre de Rádio e Televisão (Lúcio Costa, 1959)
Universidade de Brasília (1960/1968): Campus masterplan (Lúcio Costa), Instituto Central de Ciências (Oscar Niemeyer and Jao Filgueira Lima), Restaurante Universitário (José Galbinski), Biblioteca (José Galbinski, Miguel Alves Pereira, Jodete Rio Sócrates and Vaimir Aguiar), Centro Esportivo (Paulo de Melo Zimbres, Ricardo Farret and Márcio Boas), Alojamento para Estudantes Students Hostel (Leo Bonfim Jr., Solon Leao de Souza and Alberto Xavier), Edifício da Reitoria (Paulo Zimbres)

CIDADES SATÉLITES

Ceilândia (1957)
Samambaia (1957)
Taguatinga (1957)

SÃO PAULO

Agência Butantã do Banco do Estado de São Paulo (Ruy Othake, 1975)
Alphaville Residential 2 (Albuquerque, Takaoka S.A., 1976)
Alphaville Residential 9 (Albuquerque, Takaoka S.A., 1996)
Alphaville Rodovia Castello Branco (Albuquerque, Takaoka S.A., 1974)
Avenida Berrini (1978/1993)
Avenida Paulista (1890/1950)
Catedral Metropolitana (Max Hehl,

1911)
Centro Administrativo Itaú (1990)
Edifício Banespa (Carlos Brakte, 1939)
Edifício Copan (Oscar Niemeyer, 1951)
Edifício Giambe (Paulo Mendes da Rocha and João E. de Genaro, 1964)
Edifício Itália (Adolf Franz Heep, 1956)
Edifício Martinelli (Guiseppe Martinelli, 1929)
Edifício Sede IAB - Instituto de Arquitetos do Brasil (Abelardo de Souza and Rino Levi, 1947)
Estaçao de Metrô Sé (Robert Ezell, Mac Fadden and José Paulo de Bem, 1975)
Estação Ponte Pequena (Marcello Fragelli, 1968)
Faculdade de Arquitetura - Universade de São Paulo (J. Vilanova Altigas, 1961)
Jardim Europa
Largo de São Bento (1975)
Marginal Pinheiros - Marginal Tietê
MASP - Museu de Arte de São Paulo (Lina Bo Bardi, 1960)
Memorial da América Latina (Oscar Niemeyer, 1988/1995)
Morumbi, Shopping Center (1982)
MUBE - Museu Brasileiro de Escultura (Paulo Mendes da Rocha and Roberto Burle Marx, 1988/1995)
Palácio da Indústria (Oscar Niemeyer, Zenon Lofoto, Hélio Uchoa and Eduardo Kneese de Mello, 1951)
Palácio das Artes (Oscar Niemeyer, Zenon Lofoto, Hélio Uchoa and Eduardo Kneese de Mello, 1951)
Parque Ibirapuera (1954)
Praça da República (1901)
Praça da Sé (José Eduardo de Assis Lefèvre, EMURB, 1976)
SESC Fábrica da Pompéia (Lina Bo Bardi, Marcelo Ferraz and André Vainer, 1986)
Shop Forma (Paulo Mendes da Rocha, 1996)
Vale do Anhangabaú (Jorge Wilheim, Rosa Kliass and Jamil Kfouri 1992)

FOZ DO IGUAÇÚ

Itaipú Dam
Igaçú Falls

SÃO JOSÉ DOS CAMPOS

CTA - Centro Técnico de Auronáutica (Oscar Niemeyer, 1948)
Tecelagem Parahyba
Parque Municipal, former Oliv Gomes Estate (Rino Levi, Robert de Cerqueira Cesár and Robert Burle Marx, 1950/1965)

AREIAS

Fazenda Vargem Grande garden (Roberto Burle Marx, 1979)
Fazenda Pau d'Alho